The Ultimate Bodybuilding Training Program:

Increase Muscle Mass in 30 Days or Less Without Anabolic Steroids, Creatine Supplements, or Pills

By

Joseph Correa

Professional Athlete and Coach

COPYRIGHT

© 2016 Correa Media Group

All rights reserved

Reproduction or translation of any part of this work beyond that permitted by section 107 or 108 of the 1976 United States Copyright Act without the permission of the copyright owner is unlawful.

This publication is designed to provide accurate and authoritative information in regard to

The subject matter covered. It is sold with the understanding that neither the author nor the publisher is engaged in rendering medical advice. If medical advice or assistance is needed, consult with a doctor. This book is considered a guide and should not be used in any way detrimental to your health. Consult with a physician before starting make sure it's right for you.

ACKNOWLEDGEMENTS

To all the people who have supported and helped to make this book possible.

The Ultimate Bodybuilding Training Program:

Increase Muscle Mass in 30 Days or Less Without Anabolic Steroids, Creatine Supplements, or Pills

By

Joseph Correa

Professional Athlete and Coach

INTRODUCTION

For bodybuilders to develop consistent muscle growth they need to have a solid training plan and they need to supplement it with great nutrition.

This book will provide you with an organized training plan and calendar. Both a NORMAL and an INTENSE version of this training program are included in case you find the NORMAL version not challenging enough. Make sure to include the nutritional recipes suggested in your diet to see maximum muscle development. Eat right and train hard to see real results fast. The nutritional portion of this training program comes with delicious breakfast, lunch, dinner, and dessert recipes. Muscle shake recipes are also included to help increase additional muscle growth.

Bodybuilders who begin this training plan will see the following:

- Increased muscle growth
- Enhanced strength, mobility, and muscle reaction.
- Better capacity to train for long periods of time
- Faster increase of lean muscle
- Lower muscle fatigue
- Faster recovery times after competing or training

CONTENTS

COPYRIGHT

ACKNOWLEDGEMENTS

INTRODUCTION

CHAPTER 1: THE ULTIMATE BODYBUILDING TRAINING PROGRAM CALENDARS

NORMAL CALENDAR

INTENSE CALENDAR

CHAPTER 2: THE ULTIMATE BODYBUILDING TRAINING PROGRAM EXERCISES

DYNAMIC WARM-UP EXERCISES

HIGH PERFORMANCE TRAINING EXERCISES

CHAPTER 3: BODYBUILDING MUSCLE GROWTH: BREAKFAST RECIPES

CHAPTER 4: BODYBUILDING MUSCLE GROWTH: LUNCH RECIPES

CHAPTER 5: BODYBUILDING MUSCLE GROWTH: DINNER RECIPES

CHAPTER 6: BODYBUILDING MUSCLE GROWTH: DESSERT RECIPES

CHAPTER 7: HIGH PROTEIN SHAKE RECIPES TO INCREASE MUSCLE GROWTH

OTHER GREAT TITLES BY THIS AUTHOR

CHAPTER 1: THE ULTIMATE BODYBUILDING TRAINING PROGRAM CALENDARS

"NORMAL" CALENDAR

				1	2	3	4
5	6	7	8	9	10	11	
Chest & Triceps	Core	Quads & hams	Active recovery	Back & biceps	Delts	Active recovery	
12	13	14	15	16	17	18	
Chest & Triceps	Core	Quads & hams	Active recovery	Back & biceps	Delts	Active recovery	
19	20	21	22	23	24	25	
Chest & Triceps	Core	Quads & hams	Active recovery	Back & biceps	Delts	Active recovery	
26	27	28	29	30	31		
Chest & Triceps	Core	Quads & hams	Active recovery	Back & biceps	Delts	Active recovery	

"INTENSE" CALENDAR

				1	2	3	4
5	6	7	8	9	10	11
Chest & Triceps	Core	Quads & hams	Active recovery	Back & biceps	Delts	Active recovery
12	13	14	15	16	17	18
Chest & Triceps	Core	Quads & hams	Active recovery	Back & biceps	Delts	Active recovery
19	20	21	22	23	24	25
Chest & Triceps	Core	Quads & hams	Active recovery	Back & biceps	Delts	Active recovery
26	27	28	29	30	31	
Chest & Triceps	Core	Quads & hams	Active recovery	Back & biceps	Delts	Active recovery

CHAPTER 2: THE ULTIMATE BODYBUILDING TRAINING PROGRAM EXERCISES

TRAINING REGIMEN
You will be expected to complete five workouts per week for the next four weeks. These workouts have been designed to not only produce maximum muscle growth, but also to ensure that every muscle group is evenly targeted.

DON'T SKIMP ON THE RECOVERY

On days where no workout has been prescribed, you will have to complete an active recovery session in addition to a stretching routine. This is because we want to ensure that our muscles maintain optimal mobility as we put on more mass.

WHAT WILL I BE ABLE TO ACCOMPLISH AFTER THIS PROGRAM?

The purpose of the program is to work synergistically with the diet prescribed in the book in order to produce maximum growth. You can expect to get bigger, stronger and leaner.

WORKOUT FORMAT

Each week will be divided into 5 workouts referred to as "splits" in the book that target specific muscles groups. These splits will be organized as follows: chest & triceps, back & biceps, quads & hamstrings (legs), traps and delts (shoulders) and abdominals (core). Additionally, you will also be expected to perform 2 active recovery & stretching sessions on your off-days. These will cover the whole body regardless of what muscle group you just worked-out.

- ✓ **For weeks 1 and 3 complete exercises:** 1,2,7,8 for each split with the exception of shoulders for which you will always complete 1,2,3,4

- ✓ **For weeks 2 and 4 complete exercises:** 3,4,5,6 for each split with the exception of shoulders for which you will always complete 1,2,3,4

INTENSE ROUTINE

We have also taken the liberty to create an intense calendar. The splits remain the same, with the exception that sets will be doubled. You should not change the weights or the reps. You may take additional breaks in between the sets.

STRETCHING ROUTINE

These are a set of 7 stretches that the athlete will have to complete on days marked "active recovery".

1. **Complete shoulder and chest stretch:** Hold on to a pole on the squat rack or some other object with your arm fully extended. Rotate your body without out moving your arm until you feel a stretch in the chest and shoulders. Hold this position for 90 seconds. Repeat with other arm.

2. **Hanging stretch:** Hold on to a pull-up bar with your palms facing outward. Hang for 90 seconds.

3. **Triceps stretch:** Extend your arms above your head. With one arm grab the back of your neck. With the other hand crab the elbow of the bent arm and pull it toward your neck. Hold this position for 90 seconds. Repeat with the other arm.

4. **Quads stretch:** Stand in front of a wall. Put one hand on the wall and lean on it. Pull the opposite leg backward with the hand that is free so that your

foot touches your butt. Hold for 90 seconds. Repeat with the other leg.

5. **Calves stretch:** Stand one meter from the wall and let yourself fall onto it, catching yourself with both hands. You should be holding yourself at an angle to the all. Hold for 90 seconds.

6. **Hamstring stretch:** Sit on the floor and straighten one leg in front of you. Bend the opposite knee placing that foot against the thigh of your stretched leg. Reach for the stretched leg with the arm on the same side. Hold for 90 seconds. Repeat with opposite leg.

7. **Abdominal stretch:** Lie on your stomach with hands lifting your torso up (legs should be flat, torso should curve up). Hold position for 90 seconds.

ACTIVE RECOVERY SESSION

These are a set of 6 exercises that the athlete will have to complete before each workout (referred to as split in this book) in combination with 30 minutes of moderate intensity cardio. Additionally, he will also have to complete these exercises on the 3 days per week marked "active recovery" before the stretches.

1. **Rollover's into V-sits:** Start by sitting down on the floor. Next propel yourself backwards by rolling your knees inward so that they touch your chest (your weight should be on the back now) with your arms extended on the ground. Finally, roll back to forward position and spread your legs so that they form a V shape. Perform 15 times.

2. **Fire Hydrants:** Start by getting down on your knees, palms flat on the ground (shoulder width). Ensure that your back is straight. Without moving your back, draw a circle with your knee so that it moves outward, forward and back. Repeat for each leg 15 times.

3. **IT band foam rolling:** Start rolling with a foam roller below your hip down to your thighs. Perform 10-15 times. Focus specifically on the tight areas.

4. **Abductors foam rolling:** Start rolling with a foam roller below the crease of your hip and work your way up. Focus specifically on the tight areas. Perform 10-15 rolls. Focus specifically on the tight areas.
5. **Glute lacrosse ball smash:** Place tennis ball below butt. Cross the opposite leg and roll until you find a sore spot. Focus on rolling the area for 60 seconds. Repeat for other side.

6. **Groaners:** Start in a push up position. Using both legs, jump forward without moving your hands, and lading with your feet touching your hands. Jump back to push-up position. Repeat for 20 reps.

PECTORAL & TRICEP EXERCISES

These are the exercises that will condition your chest and triceps.

1. Weighted dips (triceps)

How to:

a. Use a weight strap to put an adequate amount of weight around your torso. Alternatively, hold a dumbbell between your legs.
b. Position your hands on each side of the bar so that your arms are fully extended and supporting yourself
c. Lower your body by bending at the elbow while ensuring that the movement is controlled
d. Press your body back up to starting position

Rep scheme:

***3 sets of 10-12 reps. each set should be difficult but you should not reach complete failure. You should be able to do 2-3 more reps after the 10th rep. Adjust repetition range until criteria is met but do not change the number of sets. If exercises is too difficult, perform the dips without the weight. If still too difficult, perform the exercise on a dip machine.

Health benefits:

+++Growth, ++Strength, ++Endurance

2. Weighted diamond push-ups (triceps)

How to:

a. Lie down on the floor facedown and position your hands narrower than shoulder width apart.
b. Have someone help you position an adequate weight on your back
c. Slowly lower yourself downward until chest is a fist length from the floor
d. Push yourself upward

Rep scheme:

***3 sets of 10-12 repetitions. Each set should be difficult but you should not reach complete failure. You should be able to do 2-3 more reps after the 10th rep. Adjust weight until criteria is met but do not change the number of sets or reps.

Health benefits:

+++Growth, ++Strength, ++Endurance

3. Skull crushers (triceps)

How to:

a. Grab the bar with a close grip and hold it with elbows tucked in
b. Lie down on the bench while ensuring that your arms are at a 90 degree angle
c. Without moving your arms, lower the bar
d. Lift the bar back to starting position

Rep scheme:

***3 sets of 10-12 repetitions. Each set should be difficult but you should not reach complete failure. You should be able to do 2-3 more reps after the 10th rep. Adjust weight until criteria is met but do not change the number of sets or reps.

Health benefits:

+++Growth, ++Strength, ++Endurance

4. Triceps extension (triceps)

How to:

a. Sit down on a triceps extension machine
b. Place arms against pads and grab ahold of the handles
c. Lower your arms by extending your elbows
d. Return to starting position

Rep scheme:

***3 sets of 10-12 repetitions. Each set should be difficult but you should not reach complete failure. You should be able to do 2-3 more reps after the 10th rep. Adjust weight until criteria is met but do not change the number of sets or reps.

Health benefits:

+++Growth, ++Strength, +Endurance

5. Bench press (chest)

How to:

a. Lay down on the bench with your feet flat on the floor
b. Grab the bar with a grip that is slightly wider than shoulder-width
c. Lift the bar so that it is over the center of your chest
d. Lower the bar until it touches your chest or as close to it as possible
e. Push the bar up until your arms are fully-extended
f. Repeat d-e

Rep scheme:

***3 sets of 10-12 repetitions. Each set should be difficult but you should not reach complete failure. You should be able to do 2-3 more reps after the 10th rep. Adjust weight until criteria is met but do not change the number of sets or reps.

Health benefits:

+++Growth, ++Strength, +Endurance

6. Incline bench press (chest)

How to:

a. Lay down on and incline bench with your feet flat on the floor
b. Grab the bar with a grip that is slightly wider than shoulder-width
c. Lift the bar so that it is over the center of your chest
d. Lower the bar until it touches the upper portion of your chest, or as close to it as possible
e. Push the bar up until your arms are fully-extended
f. Repeat d-e

Rep scheme:

***3 sets of 10-12 repetitions. Each set should be difficult but you should not reach complete failure. You should be able to do 2-3 more reps after the 10th rep. Adjust weight until criteria is met but do not change the number of sets or reps.

Health benefits:

+++Growth, ++Strength, +Endurance

7. Dumbbell Press (Chest)

How to:

a. Sit upright on the bench with your feet flat on the floor
b. Grab the dumbbells and put them on your thighs
c. Lie down while kicking the weights so that your arms are fully extended holding them
d. Lower the weights until it touches your chest or as close to it as possible
e. Push the weights up until your arms are fully-extended
f. Repeat d-e

Rep scheme:

***3 sets of 10-12 repetitions. Each set should be difficult but you should not reach complete failure. You should be able to do 2-3 more reps after the 10th rep. Adjust weight until criteria is met but do not change the number of sets or reps.

Health benefits:

+++Growth, ++Strength, +Endurance

8. Dumbbell flies (chest)

How to:

a. Sit up right on a flat bench, holding a dumbbell in each hand
b. Rest the weights on on your thighs
c. Lie down on the bench while using the thighs to raise the dumbbells into a pressing position
d. While your arms are fully extended, lower your arms on each side
e. Return arms to starting position while squeezing chest

Rep scheme:

***3 sets of 10-12 repetitions. Each set should be difficult but you should not reach complete failure. You should be able to do 2-3 more reps after the 10th rep. Adjust weight until criteria is met but do not change the number of sets or reps.

Health benefits:

+++Growth, ++Strength, +Endurance

DELTOID & TRAPEZOID EXERCISES

These are the exercises that will condition your shoulders.

1. Overhead barbell shoulder press (Delts)

How to:

a. Stand in front of the bar shoulder width apart
b. Ensure that the bar is at the height of your shoulders
c. Grip the bar narrower than shoulder-width apart with both hands facing outward
d. Press the bar upwards in a vertical line while slightly moving your chin back
e. Lower the bar back to starting position

Rep scheme:

***3 sets of 10 repetitions. Each set should be fairly heavy. You should be able to do 1-2 more reps after the 10th rep. Adjust weight until criteria is met but do not change the number of sets or reps.

Health benefits:

+++Strength, +++Power

2. Seated dumbbell shoulder press (delts)

How to:

a. Sit down with the weights placed on top of your thighs
b. Kick the weights by lifting your knees
c. You should be in a pressing position
d. Press the weight upward in a vertical line
e. Lower the weights back to starting position

Rep scheme:

***3 sets of 10-12 repetitions. Each set should be difficult but you should not reach complete failure. You should be able to do 2-3 more reps after the 10th rep. Adjust weight until criteria is met but do not change the number of sets or reps.

Health benefits:

+++Growth, ++Strength, +Endurance

3. Dumbbell lateral raises (delts)

How to:

a. Stand shoulder width apart with a weight in both hands
b. Lift weight on each side with palms facing down until arms are perpendicular to torso
c. Lower weights back to starting position

Rep scheme:

***3 sets of 10-12 repetitions. Each set should be difficult but you should not reach complete failure. You should be able to do 2-3 more reps after the 10th rep. Adjust weight until criteria is met but do not change the number of sets or reps.

Health benefits:

+++Growth, ++Strength, +Endurance

4. Upright row (delts)

How to:

a. Stand shoulder width apart with barbell in your hands
b. Row the barbell with palm facing inward vertically up
c. Lower the weight back to starting position

Rep scheme:

***3 sets of 10-12 repetitions. Each set should be difficult but you should not reach complete failure. You should be able to do 2-3 more reps after the 10th rep. Adjust weight until criteria is met but do not change the number of sets or reps.

Health benefits:

+++Growth, ++Strength, +Endurance

BACK & BICEP EXERCISES

These are the exercises that will condition your back and biceps.

1. Pull-up (back)

How to:

a. Grab the bar shoulder width apart with palms facing forwards.
b. As you are hanging, slightly bring your torso back to form a small incline
c. Pull your torso up until the bar touches or is close to touching the upper portion of your chest
d. Lower yourself and repeat

Rep scheme:

***3 sets of 10-12 repetitions. Each set should be difficult but you should not reach complete failure. You should be able to do 2-3 more reps after the 10th rep. Adjust weight until criteria is met but do not change the number of sets or reps.

Health benefits:

+++Growth, ++Strength, +Endurance

2. Bent-over barbell row (back)

How to:

a. Hold the barbell with palms facing inwards
b. Let the barbell hang at slightly below your waist or until your arms are fully extended
c. Bend your knees slightly and bend your torso forward while making sure that it doesn't round
d. Your head should be looking in front of you and your legs and torso should make an L shape as the barbell is still hanging
e. While keeping your torso stationary, lift the barbell toward the pit of your stomach
f. Lower the barbell to starting position

Rep scheme:

***3 sets of 10-12 repetitions. Each set should be difficult but you should not reach complete failure. You should be able to do 2-3 more reps after the 10th rep. Adjust weight until criteria is met but do not change the number of sets or reps.

Health benefits:

+++Growth, ++Strength, +Endurance

3. Renegade row (back)

How to:

a. Position two kettle bells shoulder-width apart on the floor
b. Position yourself like you would for a pushup with each hand grabbing a kettle bell
c. Perform a pushup
d. At the top of the movement, row the kettle bell as you would a barbell row movement.
e. Repeat for the other hand

Rep scheme:

***3 sets of 10-12 repetitions. Each set should be difficult but you should not reach complete failure. You should be able to do 2-3 more reps after the 10th rep. Adjust weight until criteria is met but do not change the number of sets or reps.

Health benefits:

+++Growth, ++Strength, +Endurance

4. Long bar row (back)

How to:

a. Put the weight on one side of a barbell
b. Bend over into a rowing position
c. Grab the bar with both hands on the side of the weights
d. Row the bar toward the pit of your stomach
e. Lower the bar back into starting position

Rep scheme:

***3 sets of 10-12 repetitions. Each set should be difficult but you should not reach complete failure. You should be able to do 2-3 more reps after the 10th rep. Adjust weight until criteria is met but do not change the number of sets or reps.

Health benefits:

+++Growth, ++Strength, +Endurance

5. Hammer curls (biceps)

How to:

a. Stand shoulder width apart with a dumbbell in each hand
b. Curl the weights while ensuring that the palms are facing the thighs
c. Hold for one second at the top of the squeeze
d. Lower the weights back to starting position

Rep scheme:

***3 sets of 10-12 repetitions. Each set should be difficult but you should not reach complete failure. You should be able to do 2-3 more reps after the 10th rep. Adjust weight until criteria is met but do not change the number of sets or reps.

Health benefits:

+++Growth, ++Strength, +Endurance

6. Dumbbell curls (biceps)

How to:

a. Stand shoulder width apart with a dumbbell in each hand

a. Curl the weights while ensuring that the palms are facing in front of you
b. Hold for one second at the top of the squeeze
c. Lower the weights back to starting position

Rep scheme:

***3 sets of 10-12 repetitions. Each set should be difficult but you should not reach complete failure. You should be able to do 2-3 more reps after the 10th rep. Adjust weight until criteria is met but do not change the number of sets or reps.

Health benefits:

+++Growth, ++Strength, +Endurance

7. Barbell curl (biceps)

How to:

a. Stand shoulder width apart holding a barbell with palms facing outward
b. Your hands should be positioned slightly narrower than shoulder-width apart
c. Curl the weight up holding for one second at the top
d. Lower weight back to starting position

Rep scheme:

***3 sets of 10-12 repetitions. Each set should be difficult but you should not reach complete failure. You should be able to do 2-3 more reps after the 10th rep. Adjust weight until criteria is met but do not change the number of sets or reps.

Health benefits:

+++Growth, ++Strength, +Endurance

8. Cable hammer curls (biceps)

How to:

a. Attach a rope to a pulley and set it at the lowest height
b. Stand two feet away from the pulley
c. Grab the rope and curl the weight while ensuring that elbows are tucked in
d. Lower the weight to starting position

Rep scheme:

***3 sets of 10-12 repetitions. Each set should be difficult but you should not reach complete failure. You should be able to do 2-3 more reps after the 10th rep. Adjust weight until criteria is met but do not change the number of sets or reps.

Health benefits:

+++Growth, ++Strength, +Endurance

QUADRICEPS, HAMSTRING AND CALVES EXERCISES

These are the exercises that will condition your lower body.

1. Seated leg curls (quads)

How to:

a. Sit down on the machine
b. Position the lower leg on the pad
c. Lift your legs until fully extended and hold for 1 second
d. Lower weight back to starting position

Rep scheme:

***3 sets of 10-12 repetitions. Each set should be difficult but you should not reach complete failure. You should be able to do 2-3 more reps after the 10th rep. Adjust weight until criteria is met but do not change the number of sets or reps.

Health benefits:

+++Growth, ++Strength, +Endurance

2. Weighted lunge (quads)

How to:

a. Stand shoulder width apart
b. Step right leg forward as much as possible without overdoing it
c. Bend left leg until left knee is close to touching the floor
d. Stand back up
e. Repeat with left leg (bending the right)

Rep scheme:

***3 sets of 10-12 repetitions. Each set should be difficult but you should not reach complete failure. You should be able to do 2-3 more reps after the 10th rep. Adjust weight until criteria is met but do not change the number of sets or reps.

Health benefits:

+++Growth, ++Strength, +Endurance

3. High-bar squat quads)

How to:

a. Stand with your feet shoulder width apart
b. Hold the bar using both arms on each side of the bar shoulder-width apart (the bar should be at the height of your shoulders)
c. While holding the bar, position yourself below the bar so that it rests on top of your traps
d. Stand up so that the bar's full weight rests below your traps
e. Step back and begin to lower yourself by bending at the knees
f. Explode back up until full extension of the legs

Rep scheme:

***3 sets of 10-12 repetitions. Each set should be difficult but you should not reach complete failure. You should be able to do 2-3 more reps after the 10th rep. Adjust weight until criteria is met but do not change the number of sets or reps.

Health benefits:

+++Growth, ++Strength, +Endurance

4. Close-stance squat (quads)

How to:

a. Stand with your feet as close together as possible without touching
b. Sit down by moving your hips back with your arms extended in front of you
c. Ensure that you look up & forward as you perform the squat and your back is straight
d. Stand back up with legs fully extended

Rep scheme:

***3 sets of 10-12 repetitions. Each set should be difficult but you should not reach complete failure. You should be able to do 2-3 more reps after the 10th rep. Adjust weight until criteria is met but do not change the number of sets or reps.

Health benefits:

+++Growth, ++Strength, +Endurance

5. Front squat (quads)

How to:

a. Stand shoulder width apart in front of the barbell
b. Position the weight in-between your shoulder caps and arms
c. Lift your arms and cross them so that they and your shoulder caps form a platform for the bar
d. Squat down until your quads are parallel to the floor while ensuring that your back is straight
e. Explode into back up

Rep scheme:

***3 sets of 10-12 repetitions. Each set should be difficult but you should not reach complete failure. You should be able to do 2-3 more reps after the 10th rep. Adjust weight until criteria is met but do not change the number of sets or reps.

Health benefits:

+++Growth, ++Strength, +Endurance

6. Stiff legged barbell deadlift (hamstrings)

How to:

a. Stand with your back straight and legs shoulder width apart
b. Grab the bar which is resting on the floor with palms facing down
c. Bend at your waist (bend over) until you can reach the bar
d. While ensuring that your knees aren't bent, lift the bar using your back by straightening your waist
e. Lower yourself and repeat

Rep scheme:

***3 sets of 10-12 repetitions. Each set should be difficult but you should not reach complete failure. You should be able to do 2-3 more reps after the 10th rep. Adjust weight until criteria is met but do not change the number of sets or reps.

Health benefits:

+++Growth, ++Strength, +Endurance

7. Deadlift (quads, hamstrings)

How to:

a. Stand shoulder-width apart in front of a barbell
b. Bend your knees (forward) and hold on to the bar with both hands
c. Start by posing with your legs while getting your torso into an upright position
d. You should now be standing upright with the barbell in your hands
e. Lower the weight and repeat

Rep scheme:

***3 sets of 10-12 repetitions. Each set should be difficult but you should not reach complete failure. You should be able to do 2-3 more reps after the 10th rep. Adjust weight until criteria is met but do not change the number of sets or reps.

Health benefits:

+++Growth, ++Strength, +Endurance

8. Hamstring curls (hamstrings)

How to:

a. Lay down on the machine
b. Position the upper portion of your ankles on the cushion
c. Lift your legs and hold for one second
d. Lower the weight and repeat

Rep scheme:

***3 sets of 10-12 repetitions. Each set should be difficult but you should not reach complete failure. You should be able to do 2-3 more reps after the 10th rep. Adjust weight until criteria is met but do not change the number of sets or reps.

Health benefits:

+++Growth, ++Strength, +Endurance

ABDOMINAL EXERCISES (CORE)

These are the exercises that will condition your core.

1. Dumbbell side-bend

How to:

a. Stand up while holding a dumbbell in both hands while standing shoulder width apart
b. Bend sideways at the waist
c. Repeat for the other side

Rep scheme:

3x20 bends per side

Health benefits:

++Strength, ++Endurance, +++Core stability

2. Cable crunch

How to:

a. Kneel below a pulley machine with a rope
b. Grab the rope with both hands
c. Flex your hips so as to engage your abs and lift the weight
d. Pull down with your back
e. Return to starting position

Rep scheme:

3x20 bends per side

Health benefits:

++Strength, ++Endurance, +++Core stability

3. Weighted Russian twist

How to:

a. Lie down on the floor (sit) with legs bent at the knees
b. Make sure your torso is upright so that it makes a V with your thighs
c. Extend your arms while holding a weight and twist your torso to the right as much as you can
d. Repeat by twisting to your left

Rep Scheme:

***3 sets of 20 reps. each set should be difficult but you should not reach complete failure. You should be able to do 2-3 more reps after the 20th rep. Adjust repetition range until criteria is met but do not change the number of sets.

Health benefits:

++Strength, +++Core stability

4. Leg raise

How to:

a. Lie down on the floor with your legs straight
b. Place your hands next to your glutes on each side
c. Lift your legs up to make a 90-degree angle while ensuring that your legs aren't bending (your hands should help you balance yourself and be pushing on the floor)

Rep Scheme:

***3 sets of 20 reps. each set should be difficult but you should not reach complete failure. You should be able to do 2-3 more reps after the 20th rep. Adjust repetition range until criteria is met but do not change the number of sets.

Health benefits:

++Strength, +++Core Stability

5. Crunch

How to:

a. Lie down on the floor facing up
b. Bend your knees so that they form a 90-degree angle
c. Lift your torso up just enough that your shoulders don't touch the floor (do not sit up completely)

Rep scheme:

***3 sets of 40 reps. each set should be difficult but you should not reach complete failure. You should be able to do 2-3 more reps after the 40th rep. Adjust repetition range until criteria is met but do not change the number of sets.

Health benefits:

+++Endurance, +++Core stability

6. Push-up plank

How to:

a. Position yourself in a push-up position
b. Lower yourself down so that you are in the first half of the push-up movement
c. Hold position

Rep scheme:

***3 sets of 60 seconds. Each set should be difficult but you should not reach complete failure. Adjust time but not number of sets if needed.

Health benefits:

+++Endurance, ++Core stability

7. Lying windmills hold

How to:

a. Lie down face-up with your arms extended and raise your legs so that they form a 90-degree angle
b. Hold the position

Rep scheme:

***3 sets of 60 seconds.

Health benefits:

+++Endurance, +++Strength

8. Bicycle crunch

How to:

a. Lie on your back with your hands behind your head
b. Bend your legs so that they are at a 90-degree angle
c. Bring your right knee toward the left elbow and touch if possible
d. Repeat with left knee

Rep scheme:

***3 sets of 20 reps. each set should be difficult but you should not reach complete failure. You should be able to do 2-3 more reps after the 20th rep. Adjust repetition range until criteria is met but do not change the number of sets.

Health benefits:

+++Strength, +++Endurance

CARDIOVASCULAR EXERCISES

These are the exercises that you will complete before every workout at a moderate intensity.

1. High-intensity training(HIT) sprints

How to:

The idea is to perform 8x30 second sprints at maximum intensity with 2 minutes of rest in-between each sprint.

Health benefits:

++ Power, +++Recovery, +++Speed

2. Hill sprints (HIT)

How to:

The idea is to perform 5x 10-30 second sprints on a hill or an inclined surface with 2 minutes of rest in-between each sprint.

Health benefits:

+++Power, +++Speed

GLOSSARY

Active recovery: resting your muscles while staying active so that the blood flow will accelerate your recovery

Biceps: muscles of the arm (inner region)

Delts: shoulder muscles

Traps: trapezoid muscles (below the neck)

Growth: muscle growth

Endurance: the ability to produce output over a long period of time

Failure: this is complete exhaustion, the inability to continue

Power: the ability to produce the most energy in the shortest amount of time

Quads: quadriceps muscles (thighs outer region)

Hamstrings: hamstring muscles (thighs inner region)

Strength: the ability to lift higher loads for the same volume of work

Triceps: muscles of the arms (outer region)

CHAPTER 3: BODYBUILDING MUSCLE GROWTH: BREAKFAST RECIPES

This section will provide you with specific recipes for you to prepare or have prepared in order in increase your protein consumption. You may increase the amount and protein portions as needed and can switch the order of the meals if necessary.

For example, if you prefer to have a specific dinner recipe instead of the lunch menu provided, go ahead as long as you complete at least three meals and add a protein shake included right after these meal recipes.

The dessert recipes included are up to you if you want to include them as part of your diet or not.

For best results try to have at least 5 meals a day and add a protein shake as well.

Make sure to drink plenty of water to help your body digest the high amounts of protein you will be consuming. Depending on your lifestyle and the amount of cardio you include in your training this may range from 10 to 16 glasses of water.

Breakfast recipe 1

Ricotta and peaches waffles

This wonderful and easy-to-make protein-rich breakfast will keep you full for hours and will provide all the energy needed during the day. Ricotta cheese is a wonderful source of protein and calcium.

Ingredients:

Whole-grain waffle

1 sliced peach

½ cup part-skim ricotta cheese

Preparation:

Top the waffle with cheese and sliced peach.

Cal: 300

Protein: 15g

Fat: 13g

Carb: 38g

Fiber: 6g

Breakfast recipe 2

Apple, cheese and cinnamon salad

There's nothing like a healthy and sweet breakfast to start your day with. If you don't like cinnamon, switch it for any other spice. Cottage cheese will help remove artery-clogging fat, and is packed with protein.

Ingredients:

¾ cup nonfat cottage cheese

1 sliced apple

Cinnamon

Preparation:

Simply sprinkle the cheese and cinnamon over the sliced apple.

Calories: 250

Protein: 25g

Fat: 2g

Carb: 36

Fiber: 6

Breakfast recipe 3

Breakfast Classic BLT

This is the healthiest version of the classic sandwich. It is loaded with protein that will give you enough energy for your morning workout routine.

Ingredients:

Whole-grain English muffin

Low-fat mayo

4 slices Canadian bacon or turkey bacon

Lettuce

Sliced tomato

Preparation:

Use the muffin as a base and top each half with a spread of mayo, a slice of bacon, lettuce and sliced tomato.

Calories: 205

Protein: 16g

Fat: 4g

Carb: 30g

Fiber: 3g

Breakfast recipe 4

Fruity Greek yogurt

Whenever you are craving yogurt, have in mind that the Greek version has twice as much protein as the traditional version. That's why it should be part of your morning protein-rich diet habit.

Ingredients:

Greek yogurt 6-ounce

1 tbsp toasted, chopped nuts, any kind

1-2 tbsp whole-grain cereal

½ banana

½ cup berries

1 orange

Preparation:

Top the yogurt with all ingredients and mix. Use the orange on the side.

Calories: 260

Protein: 22g

Fat: 5g

Carb: 38g

Fiber: 3g

Breakfast recipe 5

Protein-rich Western Scramble

This is a wonderful breakfast that you can make on Sunday and eat all week. It is perfect for very busy mornings and is packed with 40 grams of protein for your muscle building.

Ingredients:

5 cups egg beaters

1 cup cheddar cheese

8 oz chopped low-sodium ham

1 cup diced onion

1 diced poblano pepper

1 Tbsp olive oil

5 apples

Preparation:

Add oil to a pan over medium heat. Once oil is warmed, add peppers and onions. Sauté until onions become translucent. Combine egg beaters, ham, cheese, and peppers and onions.

Let it cool. Stir egg mixture and remove one serving, spooning it into a microwave-safe bowl. Microwave for 2 minutes, stir, and then microwave for another 30 seconds. Serve with an apple.

Calories: 418

Fat: 13g

Carbs: 35g

Fiber: 6g

Protein: 40g

Breakfast recipe 6

1-Minute Ham & Egg

This simple yet very healthy breakfast bowl will keep you full until lunch. It is best served while really hot. Who would've thought that a classic dish like this could help you build muscles?

Ingredients:

1 thin slice deli ham

1 beaten egg

Shredded Cheddar cheese

Preparation:

Line the bottom of custard cup with ham. Pour egg over ham. Microwave on high for 30 seconds then stir. Microwave for 15 to 30 seconds. Top with cheese. Serve while hot.

Calories: 133

Total Fat: 8 g

Sodium: 420 mg

Carbohydrates: 2 g

Protein: 12 g

Breakfast recipe 7

Bacon and Egg Breakfast

Another healthy egg recipe to keep you satisfied until lunch time. Most of the people enjoy every ingredient, so there is no reason to make it your morning routine.

Ingredients:

2 Eggs

2 Tbsp. milk or water

Salt and pepper

3 tsp. butter

4 slices whole wheat bread

2 slices cheese

4 slices cooked bacon

Preparation:

Beat eggs, milk, salt and pepper. Heat 1 tsp. butter over medium heat until hot. Pour in egg mixture. Gently pull the eggs across the pan with an inverted turner, forming large curds. Continue pulling and folding eggs until thickened. Remove from pan.

Spread remaining 2 tsp. butter evenly on one side of each bread slice. Place 2 slices in skillet, buttered side down. Top evenly with scrambled eggs, cheese and bacon. Cover with remaining bread, buttered side up.

Grill sandwiches turning once, until bread is toasted and cheese is melted.

Calories: 408

Total Fat: 23 g

Cholesterol: 239 mg

Sodium: 698 mg

Carbohydrates: 24 g

Dietary Fiber: 4 g

Protein: 23 g

Breakfast recipe 8

Berry Smoothie

There's nothing tastier than a sweet breakfast early in the morning. It takes only 2 minutes to prepare it, and it will keep you full for hours.

Ingredients:

¾ cup skim milk or non-fat milk

½ banana

6 ounce nonfat Greek yogurt

¾ berries, fresh or frozen

Ice cubes

Preparation:

Mix all the ingredients in a blender until smooth. Enjoy.

Calories: 265

Protein: 25 g

Fat: 1 g

Carbs: 40 g

Fiber: 4 g

Breakfast recipe 9

Veggie garden omelet

This colorful dish is packed with protein and very low in fat. It is easy to make and you can substitute vegetables with fruits or vice versa.

Ingredients:

Omelet of 1 egg and 2 to 3 egg whites

Handful of spinach, peppers, mushroom, zucchini, onions, tomatoes (or just one)

Seasoning

Basil

Whole-grain toast

Almonds, cashew or peanut butter

Whip the omelet and then add the vegetables, chopped basil, and seasoning. Enjoy with a toast and almonds, cashew or peanut butter – for healthy fat.

Calories: 280

Protein: 27 g

Fat: 9 g

Carbs: 26 g

Fiber: 5 g

Breakfast recipe 10

Meal replacement breakfast shake

This shake is your best friend after a rigorous workout routine. If you want to cut on the fat, go without peanut butter.

Ingredients

1/2 chopped banana

1/2 cup of chopped strawberries

1 apple

1 plum

2 tbsp of wheat germ

1 cup of non-fat milk

optional 1 tbsp of peanut butter

Preparation:

Place chopped banana, apple, strawberries and plum in blender. Add nonfat milk and wheat germ. Add peanut butter (optional). Place a couple of cubes of ice in the blender. Serve.

Calories: 705

Fat: 21.3 g

Sodium: 177.1 mg

Total Carbs: 101.8 g

Dietary Fiber: 22.8 g

Protein: 43.2 g

Breakfast recipe 11

10-Minute Breakfast Pita

It is easy to make and very filling! Tastes delicious and is packed with protein.

Ingredients:

Sliced Jalapenos

one pita

5 sprays of butter spray

2 slices of American nonfat cheese

sliced tomato

one large egg

Preparation:

Spray pita on both sides with butter spray. Place 1 cooked egg on top. Put Jalapenos, tomato and 1 slice of cheese, and finish with one layer of pita. Bake in toaster at 400 for 10 minutes.

Calories: 240.1

Total Fat: 6.1 g

Cholesterol: 212.5 mg

Sodium: 339.8 mg

Total Carbs: 29.8 g

Fiber: 9.3 g

Protein: 23.5 g

Breakfast recipe 12

Breakfast pancakes

There are healthier versions of pancakes, and this is one of those. Fast and easy to make, they will give you enough energy for even the most exhausting workout.

Ingredients:

1 container non-fat Greek yogurt

6 egg whites

2/3 cup old fashioned oats

3 teaspoons sugar

1 tablespoon unsweetened cocoa powder

Preparation:

Blend eggs and yogurt. Mix oatmeal with cocoa powder. Spray pan with non-stick spray and coat the pan. When you see bubbles break on top, flip the pancake.

Calories: 35.5

Total Fat: 0.3 g

Cholesterol: 0.0 mg

Sodium: 37.1 mg

Total Carbs: 6.5 g

Fiber: 0.9 g

Protein: 23.8 g

CHAPTER 4: BODYBUILDING MUSCLE GROWTH: LUNCH RECIPES

Lunch recipe 1

Chicken Vegetable Casserole

This is the healthiest version of a crowd-pleasing traditional lunch. Everything is fresh and healthy, so there's no need for instant soups or gravies.

Ingredients:

12 oz diced cooked chicken breasts
2 T flour
2 T butter
10 oz skim milk
white pepper
1 t Italian seasoning
1 T grated parmesan cheese
7 oz penne pasta
2 yellow or orange chopped bell peppers
1 chopped zucchini
2 heads chopped broccoli,
1/3 c Monterey jack cheese
nonstick cooking spray

Preparation:

Place the butter in a small sauce pot preheated over medium heat. Once the butter foams, add flour and stir for 1 minute. Add milk and continue to stir until bubbly.

Reduce heat and simmer for 10 minutes. Add pepper, seasoning and cheese. Stir to combine. Cook pasta according to package directions. Preheat oven to 350 degrees. During the last minute of the pasta's cooking, add the broccoli to the water. Allow to simmer.

Drain the pasta and broccoli. Spray the bottom and sides of a 9 X 13 oven-proof dish with nonstick cooking spray. In a bowl, combine the pasta and broccoli with the chicken and vegetables; cover with sauce. Place in the baking dish. Sprinkle with the Monterey jack cheese and cover with foil.

Bake for 20 minutes; remove foil and bake until cheese is melted.

Calories: 320.6

Total Fat: 8.9 g

Cholesterol: 51.8 mg

Sodium: 175.3 mg

Total Carbs: 36.1 g

Dietary Fiber: 8.8 g

Protein: 27.9 g

Lunch recipe 2

BBQ Chicken Flatbreads

This family recipe is great for hot summer days and it is packed with protein. If you are craving pizza, but also want to stay in good shape, this is a great substitute.

Ingredients:

2 flatbreads
1 red onion, sliced
1 yellow or red bell pepper, sliced
Pinch black pepper
12 ounces boneless skinless chicken breast
1/4 cup barbeque sauce
1 tablespoon pineapple juice
1/4 cup chopped pineapple
1/4 cup shredded Monterey Jack
2 slices chopped Canadian bacon

Preparation:

Preheat the grill to 500 degrees Fahrenheit.
Place the onions and peppers on a large sheet of heavy-duty foil, then sprinkle with pepper.

Coat both sides of the chicken with cooking spray. Place the vegetables and chicken on the grill. Cook the chicken three or four minutes per side.

Remove the chicken and veggies from the grill, then lower the heat to 400 degrees Fahrenheit.

Cut chicken into bite-size pieces. Add the grilled veggies, barbecue sauce and pineapple juice to a blender and pulse.

Place the flatbreads on a pizza stone. Spread 1/2 cup sauce on each flatbread and top with the chicken, cheese, pineapple, and bacon and place on the grill. Cook for 10 minutes, until the cheese has melted.
Remove from heat.

Calories: 233.4

Total Fat: 5.1 g

Cholesterol: 61.5 mg

Sodium: 234.2 mg

Total Carbs: 21.4 g

Dietary Fiber: 2.9 g

Protein: 25.8 g

Lunch recipe 3

Mexican Casserole

This is one the family favorites! It is healthy, spicy and packed with protein.

Ingredients:

1 can fat free cream mushroom soup
1 can fat free cream chicken soup
2 cans water
1 can drained and rinsed black beans
1 can diced tomatoes
1 1/2 c instant rice
1 pkg taco seasoning
cilantro and green onions chopped
3 pounds frozen boneless, skinless chicken breasts
1 cup shredded cheddar cheese

Preparation:

Preheat the oven to 350.
Coat a 13x9 inch casserole dish with cooking spray. In a bowl, whisk together the soups, water and taco seasoning, then pour into the dish. Sprinkle the rice, then place the chicken breasts (still frozen) on top.
Pour the beans and tomatoes over the chicken, sprinkle on the cilantro and green onions.

Cover with foil and bake for 1 hour, 40 minutes. Remove foil, sprinkle shredded cheese over to melt and bake for another 10 minutes.

Calories: 269.9

Total Fat: 5.1 g

Cholesterol: 79.3 mg

Sodium: 546.4 mg

Total Carbs: 19.3 g

Dietary Fiber: 3.8 g

Protein: 34.4 g

Lunch recipe 4

Protein-rich vegan chili

There's no reason for vegan meals to be bland. This wonderful chili is free of dairy and meat, but still tastes delicious.

Ingredients:

4 cans tomato sauce
1 can of Pinto Beans
1 cubed Vidalia onion
One package of ground crumbles
1 square of 72% cocoa chocolate
2 TBS of chili powder
1 TBS of black pepper
0.5 tsp cinnamon
0.5 tsp nutmeg

Preparation:

In a non-stick pan sauté the crumbles and the diced onion until onion is soft. Then, combine all the ingredients in a slow cooker and cook on high for 3 hours, then switch to low until ready to serve.

Calories: 348.2

Total Fat: 3.0 g

Cholesterol: 0.0 mg

Sodium: 2,408.5 mg

Total Carbs: 44.7 g

Dietary Fiber: 18.6 g

Protein: 56.9 g

Lunch recipe 5

White beans soup

This simple and easy recipe for summer lunch is packed with 80 grams of protein. It is delicious and can be made with almost anything you can find in your fridge.

Ingredients:

2 - skinless, boneless chicken breasts cut into bite size pieces
2 carrots sliced
7 stalks of celery sliced
1 large onion diced
1/4 c dry navy beans
1/4 c dry garbanzo
1/4 c raw dry pearl barley
1/4 c raw brown rice
1/4 c raw wild rice (uncooked)
1/4 c raw farro
1/4 c raw quinoa
Sea salt, pepper & parsley to taste
Water

Preparation:

Add 2 cups of water to a soup pot. Add all other ingredients and turn burner to high to start boiling. Add more water to fill pot. Bring to boil. Put lid on and turn burner down to a strong simmer. Remove lid and stir. If the water boils down, add more water to bring the level back up. Continue cooking until all beans are done. This should take about 3 hours.

Calories: 116

Total Fat: 1.9 g

Cholesterol: 21 mg

Sodium: 70 mg

Total Carbs: 15 g

Fiber: 3 g

Protein: 10.9 g

Lunch recipe 6

Mexican tuna salad

When you are in hurry and you are craving a fresh meal, don't think any further. This amazing salad is healthy and packed in protein to help you build muscles.

Ingredients:

1 large chopped onion
2 large tomatoes
bunch of cilantro
400 grams of Tuna
juice from 1 lime

Preparation:

Chop the onion and cover in salt. Cover the salted onions in water. Let them sit for 30 minutes. After they have soaked, drain them and rinse with running water.

Chop the tomatoes and cilantro and mix with the onions. Squeeze juice over. Open and drain the can of tuna and add to the mixture. Flake the tuna into bit sized pieces and toss the ingredients.

Calories: 308.8

Total Fat: 2.5 g

Cholesterol: 60.0 mg

Sodium: 695.3 mg

Total Carbs: 18.5 g

Dietary Fiber: 4.3 g

Protein: 53.7 g

Lunch recipe 7

Mediterranean fish

Add some sea taste to your feast with this beautiful baked fish. It is made with ingredients that reduce the fat, so you can enjoy it endlessly.

Ingredients:

2 teaspoon olive oil
1 large sliced onion
1 can whole tomatoes, drained and coarsely chopped
1 bay leaf
1 minced clove garlic
3/4 cup apple juice
1/2 cup reserved tomato juice
1/4 cup lemon juice
1/4 cup orange juice
1 tablespoon fresh grated orange peel
1 teaspoon crushed fennel seeds
1/2 teaspoon crushed dried oregano
1/2 teaspoon crushed dried thyme
1/2 teaspoon crushed dried basil
Black pepper to taste
1 lb. fish fillets
Preparation:

Heat oil in skillet. Add onion, and sauté until soft. Add all remaining ingredients except fish. Simmer uncovered for 30 minutes. Arrange fish in 10x6" baking dish; cover with sauce. Bake at 375º F about 15 minutes until fish flakes easily.

Calories: 225.5

Total Fat: 4.4 g

Cholesterol: 77.5 mg

Sodium: 277.0 mg

Total Carbs: 17.3 g

Dietary Fiber: 2.5 g

Protein: 29.4 g

Lunch recipe 8

Moroccan chicken

With almost no fat, this Moroccan traditional chicken is so healthy that you can feel it! There's almost no effort in making it, so it is a delight for your busy days.

Ingredients:

2 cups chopped carrots
1.5 cups dried lentils
2 lb.s boneless, skinless chicken breast halves
2 tbs. minced garlic
3/4 tsp. salt
3/4 tsp. turmeric
1/2 tsp cayenne
1/2 tsp cinnamon
4 cups of fat free chicken broth

Preparation:

Place all ingredients in the same order in crock pot. Cover and cook for 5 hours.

Calories: 355

Total Fat: 2 g

Cholesterol: 87 mg

Sodium: 763 mg

Total Carbs: 32 g

Dietary Fiber: 16 g

Protein: 49 g

Lunch recipe 9

Marinated Chicken Breasts

This is children favorite. Breasts marinated like this can be frozen and then simply thawed when you wish!

Ingredients:

1 c buttermilk
1 Tbsp. Dijon Mustard
1 Tbsp. honey
1 Tbsp. fresh rosemary
1/2 tsp dried thyme
1/2 tsp dried sage
1/2 tsp dried marjoram
1/2 tsp pepper
1 tsp salt
8 boneless chicken breasts

Preparation:

Mix buttermilk, mustard, honey, and seasonings, and pour it over chicken breasts in a freezer bag. Grill over medium heat until juices run clear.

Calories: 282.8

Total Fat: 3.2 g

Cholesterol: 138.1 mg

Sodium: 521.5 mg

Total Carbs: 3.9 g

Dietary Fiber: 0.1 g

Protein: 55.6 g

Lunch recipe 10

White beans tuna salad

This is a refreshing makeover of your favorite tuna salad. If made with tomatoes and cucumber, it is a wonderful light lunch packed with protein.

Ingredients:

2 cans chunk light tuna in water
1 can white beans or chick peas
1 diced red bell pepper
1/4 cup diced red onion
1 tbsp. olive oil
juice of 1 lemon

Parsley, tomatoes, cucumber

Preparation:

Mix everything and cool in the refrigerator for at least 4 hours. Serve on a bed of greens with cucumber and tomatoes.

Calories: 219.1

Total Fat: 4.1 g

Cholesterol: 24.7 mg

Sodium: 421.6 mg

Total Carbs: 20.4 g

Dietary Fiber: 6.1 g

Protein: 27.6 g

Lunch recipe 11

Turkey meatloaf

Meatloaf is a well-adored lunch meal for all generation. However, here we give you a healthy version of a meatloaf that is so irresistible.

Ingredients:

2lbs Ground turkey
1-pkg Stove Top Stuffing Mix
1 large egg
1/2c. Filtered water
1/4c. Ketchup

Preparation:

Preheat oven to 350 degrees. Mix all the ingredients, but omit 1/8c. Ketchup. Make a loaf and place in a baking dish. Glaze top with remaining ketchup and bake on 350 degrees for 45-55 minutes.

Calories: 220.6

Total Fat: 2.7 g

Cholesterol: 72.1 mg

Sodium: 445.2 mg

Total Carbs: 13.3 g

Dietary Fiber: 0.4 g

Protein: 28.5 g

Lunch recipe 12

Easy-to-make chicken creole

This traditional Southern dish had no added fats, and it's super easy and fast to make.

Ingredients:

Nonstick cooking spray

4 medium chicken breast halves, skinned, boned, and cut into strips

1 can (14 oz.) tomatoes

1 cup low-sodium chili sauce

1-1/2 cups green peppers

1/2 cup chopped celery

1/4 cup chopped onion

2 cloves minced garlic

1 tablespoon fresh basil

1 tablespoon fresh parsley

1/4 teaspoon crushed red pepper

1/4 teaspoon salt

Preparation:

Spray a skillet with nonstick spray. Preheat over high heat. Cook chicken stirring, for 3-5 minutes. Reduce heat. Add tomatoes and juice, chili sauce, green pepper, celery, onion, garlic, basil, parsley, red pepper, and salt. Bring to boiling; reduce heat and simmer for 10 minutes. Serve over hot cooked rice or pasta.

Calories: 255.4

Total Fat: 4.5 g

Cholesterol: 77.0 mg

Sodium: 652.4 mg

Total Carbs: 20.7 g

Dietary Fiber: 4.3 g

Protein: 33.3 g

The Ultimate Bodybuilding Training Program

CHAPTER 5: BODYBUILDING MUSCLE GROWTH: DINNER RECIPES

Dinner recipe 1

Bean Salad

This is much more than a salad. It is perfect for dinner parties when you need to plan ahead.

Ingredients:

6 slices bacon

3 15.5-ounce cans

Cannellini beans, rinsed

3 tablespoons apple cider vinegar

3 tablespoons olive oil

3 tablespoons whole-grain mustard

Kosher salt and black pepper

3 tablespoons

Chopped fresh chives

Cook the bacon in a large skillet over medium heat until crisp; crumble, cover, and set aside at room temperature. Toss the beans, vinegar, oil, and mustard and season with ½ teaspoon each salt and pepper. Refrigerate for 8 hours. Before serving, toss with the chives and bacon.

Calories 138

Fat 7 g

Sat Fat 1 g

Cholesterol 5 mg

Sodium 416 mg

Protein 5 g

Carbohydrate 13 g

Sugar 0 g

Fiber 3 g

Iron 1 mg

Calcium 28 mg

Dinner recipe 2

Turkey cutlets with peppers and beans

This recipe is for a family-pleasing dinner that will make up for all your spent protein during the day!

Ingredients:

2 tablespoons olive oil

8 turkey cutlets (about 1 1/2 pounds), pounded

Kosher salt and black pepper

2 medium thinly sliced bell peppers

2 large shallots, sliced

1 15.5-ounce can cannellini beans, rinsed

1/2 cup pitted Kalamata olives

1/2 cup

Fresh flat-leaf parsley leaves

1 tablespoon red wine vinegar

Heat 1 tablespoon of the oil in a large skillet over medium heat. Season the turkey with ¼ teaspoon salt and black pepper. Working in 2 batches, cook the turkey until cooked through, 2 to 3 minutes per side.

Heat the tablespoon of oil in a second large skillet over medium-high heat. Add the bell peppers, shallots, ½ teaspoon salt, and ¼ teaspoon black pepper. Cook until softened, 5 to 7 minutes. Add the beans, olives, parsley, and vinegar to the skillet and combine. Serve the turkey topped with the vegetable mixture.

Calories 414

Fat 20 g

Sat Fat 5 g

Cholesterol 97 mg

Sodium 755 mg

Protein 40 g

Carbohydrate 16 g

Sugar 2 g

Fiber 4 g

Iron 3 mg

Calcium 79 mg

Dinner recipe 3

Steak with skillet tomatoes

Let's admit, we all love steak. This is so delicious, it will melt every single taste bud.

Ingredients:

Kosher salt and black pepper

3 tablespoons plus 3 teaspoons olive oil

2 strip steaks (1 inch thick; about 1 1/2 pounds total)

2 pints grape tomatoes

1/4 cup fresh oregano leaves

1 pound green beans, trimmed

2 cloves garlic, thinly sliced

1/4 to 1/2 teaspoon crushed red pepper

Bring a large pot of salted water to a boil. Heat 2 teaspoons of the oil in a skillet over medium-high heat. Season the steaks with ½ teaspoon salt and ¼ teaspoon black pepper and cook to the desired doneness per side for medium-rare. Rest for 5 minutes before slicing.

Wipe out the skillet and heat 1 teaspoon of the remaining oil over medium-high heat. Add the tomatoes and ¼ teaspoon each salt and black pepper. Cook until beginning to soften, 4 to 6 minutes. Mix in the oregano.

Meanwhile, cook the green beans until tender, 3 to 4 minutes, and then drain. Wipe out the pot and heat the garlic in the remaining 3 tablespoons of oil over medium heat, stirring, until fragrant, 1 to 2 minutes. Add beans, ½ teaspoon salt, and ¼ teaspoon black pepper and combine. Sprinkle with the red pepper and serve with the steak and tomatoes.

Calories 325

Fat 13 g

Sat Fat 4 g

Cholesterol 74 mg

Sodium 863 mg

Protein 37 g

Carbohydrate 15 g

Sugar 4 g

Fiber 6 g

Iron 4 mg

Calcium 86 mg

Dinner recipe 4

Bean and spinach enchiladas

Add some Mexican spirit to your feast with this summery recipe!

Ingredients

1 15.5-ounce black beans

1 10-ounce package chopped spinach

1 cup corn

1/2 teaspoon ground cumin

8 ounces sharp Cheddar

Kosher salt and black pepper

2 16-ounce jars salsa

8 6-inch corn tortillas, warm

1 medium head romaine lettuce

4 radishes, cut

1/2 cup grape tomatoes

1/2 cucumber, sliced

3 tablespoons

Fresh lime juice

2 tablespoons

Olive oil

Sliced scallions

In a medium bowl, mash half the beans. Add the spinach, corn, cumin, 1 cup of the Cheddar, the remaining beans, ½ teaspoon salt, and ¼ teaspoon pepper and mix to combine.

Spread 1 jar of the salsa in the bottom of a slow cooker. Dividing evenly, roll up the bean mixture in the tortillas and place the rolls seam-side down in a single layer in the slow cooker. Top with the remaining salsa and Cheddar.

Cover and cook until heated through, on low for 2½ to 3 hours.

Before serving, toss the lettuce, radishes, tomatoes, and cucumber in a large bowl with the lime juice, oil, and ½ teaspoon each salt and pepper. Serve with the enchiladas and sprinkle with the scallions.

Calories 576

Fat 28 g

Sat Fat 11 g

Cholesterol 61 mg

Sodium 2,457 mg

Protein 28 g

Carbohydrate 60 g

Sugar 10 g

Fiber 12 g

Iron 4 mg

Calcium 621 mg

Dinner recipe 5

Spanish omelet with potatoes and chorizo

This wonderful omelet can be your breakfast or dinner. Either way, it is full of nutrients and good flavor!

Ingredients:

3 tablespoons

Extra-virgin olive oil

1 large yellow onion

2 ounces Spanish sausage, sliced into thin half-moons

3/4 pound red potatoes

Kosher salt and pepper

3/4 cup flat-leaf parsley, chopped

10 beaten large eggs

1 cup shredded Cheddar

1 small head green-leaf lettuce

1/2 small red onion, thinly sliced

Preheat oven to 400° F. Heat 1 tablespoon of the oil in a large skillet over medium heat. Add the yellow onion and cook for 5 minutes. Add the chorizo, potatoes, and ½ teaspoon each salt and pepper and cook, covered, stirring occasionally, until the potatoes are tender, for 10 minutes.

Add the parsley. Pour in the eggs and stir to distribute the ingredients. Sprinkle with the cheese and transfer to oven.

Bake the omelet until puffed and brown around the edges and a knife comes out clean, about 15 minutes.

Divide the lettuce and red onion among plates and drizzle with the remaining oil. Cut the omelet into wedges and serve with the salad.

Protein 29 g

Carbohydrate 23 g

Sugar 5 g

Fiber 4 g

Fat 37 g

Sat Fat 12 g

Sodium 804 mg

Cholesterol 572 mg

Dinner recipe 6

Slow-cooked corned beef and cabbage

If you have a big family, this will please them all. This amazing recipe is a classic from Balkan grandmas.

Ingredients:

4 fresh thyme sprigs

1 teaspoon caraway seeds

1 3-pound piece corned beef brisket

1 pound carrots, cut in half crosswise

1/2 small green cabbage

1 pound small red potatoes

Mustard

Combine the thyme, caraway seeds, beef (cut in half to fit if necessary) with spice packet, carrots, cabbage, potatoes, and ½ cup water in a 5- to 6-quart slow cooker. Cook, covered, until the beef is tender, on low for 7 to 8 hours or on high for 4 to 5 hours (this will shorten total recipe time).

Transfer the beef to a cutting board and thinly slice.

Serve warm with the carrots, cabbage, potatoes, and mustard, sprinkled with fresh thyme leaves.

Calories 676

Fat 39 g

Sat Fat 13 g

Cholesterol 197 mg

Sodium 2393 mg

Protein 42 g

Carbohydrate 39

Sugar 11 g

Fiber 9 g

Iron 6 mg

Calcium 151 mg

Dinner recipe 7

Shrimp risotto

Rice and shrimp, sounds delicious. There are many variations, but this one is the healthiest!

Ingredients:

4 tablespoons (1/2 stick) unsalted butter

1 small bulb fennel, chopped, plus 2 tablespoons fennel fronds, roughly chopped

1 small onion, chopped

2 cups rice

3/4 cup dry white wine

Kosher salt and black pepper

8 cups low-sodium chicken broth, warmed

1 pound peeled and deveined large shrimp

1 1/2 ounces Parmesan

Melt 2 tablespoons of the butter in a large pot or Dutch oven over medium heat. Add the fennel and onion. Cook until soft, 8 to 12 minutes.

Add the rice and stir until combined. Add the wine, ¾ teaspoon salt, and ¼ teaspoon pepper. Cook until the wine is evaporated, 1 to 2 minutes. Add 1 cup of the broth at a time and simmer, stirring occasionally until the rice is tender, 20 to 25 minutes.

Add the shrimp and cook until opaque throughout, 4 minutes. Remove from heat and stir in the Parmesan and the remaining 2 tablespoons of butter.

Serve warm topped with the fennel fronds.

Calories 440

Fat 12 g

Sat Fat 7 g

Cholesterol 144 mg

Sodium 705 mg

Protein 26 g

Carbohydrate 56 g

Sugar 2 g

Fiber 4 g

Iron 2 mg

Calcium 150 mg

Dinner recipe 8

Light chicken with goat cheese

Many people don't enjoy the taste of goat cheese. This recipe is for them – make this for you doubtful friends, and it will become their favorite!

Ingredients:

1 cup orzo

1/3 cup plus 1 tablespoon olive oil

1/4 cup chopped fresh flat-leaf parsley

1/4 teaspoon crushed red pepper

2 ounces goat cheese

4 6-ounce boneless, skinless chicken breasts

Kosher salt and black pepper

Cook the orzo according to the package directions.

Meanwhile, in a small bowl, combine ⅓ cup of the olive oil, the parsley, and crushed red pepper; fold in the goat cheese.

Season the chicken with ½ teaspoon salt and ¼ teaspoon pepper. In a large skillet, heat the remaining tablespoon of oil over medium-high heat. Working in batches, cook the chicken until cooked through, 2 to 3 minutes per side. Serve with the orzo and goat cheese vinaigrette.

Calories from fat 269

Fat 30 g

Sat Fat 7 g

Cholesterol 105 mg

Sodium 400 mg

Protein 44 g

Carbohydrate 36 g

Sugar 2 g

Fiber 2 g

Iron 3 mg

Calcium 73 mg

Dinner recipe 9

Squash lasagna

There are many ways to prepare squash, but have you ever tried lasagna? This is your chance to fall in love with this wonderful veggie.

Ingredients:

2 10- to 12-ounce packages frozen winter squash puree, thawed

1/8 teaspoon ground nutmeg

1 32-ounce container ricotta

1 5-ounce package baby spinach

Kosher salt and black pepper

12 lasagna noodles

8 ounces mozzarella

Green salad, for serving

In a bowl, mix the squash and nutmeg. In a second bowl, combine the ricotta, spinach, ½ teaspoon salt, and ¼ teaspoon pepper.

In the bottom of a 5- to 6-quart slow cooker, spread ½ cup of the squash mixture. Top with 3 of the lasagna noodles, half the remaining squash mixture, 3 lasagna noodles, and half the ricotta mixture; repeat, ending with the ricotta mixture. Sprinkle with the mozzarella. Cook on low, covered, until the noodles are tender, 3 to 4 hours. Serve with the green salad, if desired.

Calories 571

Fat 29 g

Sat Fat 18 g

Cholesterol 107 mg

Sodium 564 mg

Protein 32 g

Carbohydrate 47 g

Sugar 2 g

Fiber 6 g

Iron 3 mg

Calcium 543 mg

Dinner recipe 10

Double -beef chili

Even though this may sound like it's a masculine dish, it is very tender, but still strong and full of nutrients!

Ingredients:

2 tablespoons olive oil
1 large white onion, chopped
4 cloves garlic, chopped
Kosher salt and black pepper
1 pound ground beef chuck
1 tablespoon chili powder
1 to 3 teaspoons chopped chipotles in adobo sauce
1 12-ounce beef broth
1 28-ounce peeled tomatoes
1 15.5-ounce kidney beans
Corn bread, sour cream, cilantro, and pickled jalapeños, for serving

Heat the oil in a large saucepan over medium- high heat. Add the onion, garlic, and ½ teaspoon each salt and pepper. Cook, stirring often, until softened, 6 to 8 minutes. Add the beef and cook, breaking it up with a spoon, until no longer pink, 4 to 5 minutes more.

Add the chili powder and chipotles to the saucepan and cook, stirring, for 1 minute. Add the broth and cook until reduced by half, 6 to 8 minutes more. Add the tomatoes (with their juices), beans, and ¼ teaspoon each salt and pepper. Simmer, until thickened, 20 to 25 minutes. Serve with the corn bread, sour cream, cilantro, and pickled jalapeños.

Calories 431

Fat 21 g

Sat Fat 6 g

Cholesterol 67 mg

Sodium 956 mg

Protein 27 g

Carbohydrate 26 g

Sugar 9 g

Fiber 6 g

Iron 5 mg

Calcium 78 mg

Dinner recipe 11

Lamb meatball and Swiss stew

Add some European flavor to your feast with this amazingly delicious meatball recipe. Lamb is tender and moist; it will melt in your mouth!

Ingredients:

2 large eggs, lightly beaten
2 cloves garlic, finely chopped
3/4 cup bread crumbs
1 teaspoon sweet paprika
3/4 teaspoon cumin seeds, crushed
Kosher salt and black pepper
1 pound ground lamb
2 tablespoons olive oil
1 large bunch Swiss chard (about 11 ounces total), stems chopped and leaves sliced
6 cups low-sodium chicken broth
1/2 cup orzo or another small pasta
Plain yogurt, for serving

Combine the eggs, garlic, bread crumbs, paprika, cumin, 1¼ teaspoons salt, and ¼ teaspoon pepper in a medium bowl. Add the lamb and gently mix with your hands until just combined. Form the mixture into 18 meatballs (about 2 tablespoons each).

Heat the oil in a large pot medium-high heat. Cook the meatballs, turning occasionally, until browned all over, 4 to 6 minutes. Transfer to a plate; reserve the pot.

Add the chard stems to the reserved pot. Cook, until crisp-tender, 2 to 3 minutes. Add the chicken broth and meatballs and bring to a boil. Reduce heat and simmer until the meatballs are cooked through, 10 to 12 minutes. Add the orzo and simmer until tender, 8 to 11 minutes.

Just before serving, fold in the chard leaves. Serve warm topped with the yogurt, if desired.

Calories 365

Fat 19 g

Sat Fat 6 g

Cholesterol 131 mg

Sodium 630 mg

Protein 25 g

Carbohydrate 25 g

Sugar 3 g

Fiber 3 g

Iron 3 mg

Calcium 104 mg

Dinner recipe 12

Beef and egg burger

This is a healthy twist on your classic burger. One of children favorites.

Ingredients:

2 teaspoons canola oil, plus more for the grate
1 1/4 pounds ground beef chuck
4 slices turkey, chopped
Kosher salt and black pepper
4 English muffins, split
4 large eggs
1 large tomato, sliced

Heat grill to medium-high. Once it is hot, clean the grill grate with a brush. Oil the grill grate.

Gently mix together the beef, turkey, and ½ teaspoon each salt and pepper with your hands in a medium bowl until just combined. Form the beef mixture into four ¾-inch-thick patties. Use your fingers to make a shallow well in the top of each patty (this will prevent over plumping during cooking).

Grill the burgers until an instant-read thermometer inserted in the center registers 140° F, 4 minutes per side for medium-rare. Grill the muffins, split-side down, until toasted, 10 to 20 seconds. Heat the oil in a large nonstick skillet on the stovetop over medium heat. Crack the eggs into the skillet and cook, covered, for 2 to 3 minutes for slightly runny yolks. Season with ¼ teaspoon each salt and pepper.

Stack the tomato, burgers, and eggs between the muffins.

For maximum safety, the U.S. Department of Agriculture recommends: 165° F for poultry, 145° F for fish, and 160° F for ground beef, lamb, and turkey.

Calories 558

Fat 31 g

Sat Fat 10 g

Cholesterol 302 mg

Sodium 940 mg

Protein 40 g

Carbohydrate 28 g

Sugar 3 g

Fiber 2 g

Iron 6 mg

Calcium 226 mg

CHAPTER 6: BODYBUILDING MUSCLE GROWTH: DESSERT RECIPES

Dessert recipe 1

Raspberry muffin

This wonderful muffin can be made with any fruit you can find, but raspberries are something special to us!

Ingredients:

1 cup oats
1 tsp. cinnamon
1/2 tsp. salt
1/2 tsp. baking powder
3/4 cup low fat cottage cheese
1 egg
1/4 cup almond milk
2/3 cup raspberries
2-3 dates

Preheat your oven to 350 F. Blend all ingredients together except for the raspberries. Remove the pits from the dates before blending.

Add the raspberries and stir, and then scoop the mixture into silicon muffin cups like these ones or paper liners that have been lightly sprayed.

Place in the oven and cook for 30 to 35 minutes, or until lightly browned. If the tops of the muffins split, don't worry, they'll reform when they cool.

Calories: 90
Protein: 8g
Carbs: 10g
Fat: 2g
Fiber: 1.5g

Dessert recipe 2

Cake batter mousse

This is a perfect example of how something that is used for making cakes can be an amazing stand-alone sweet! Enjoy!

Ingredients:

2 oz. (57 g) Greek Yogurt
1 tsp. non-sweetened cocoa powder
0.5 cup Almond milk
0.7 oz. Oats
Almonds & Berries

Blend yogurt, protein powder, cocoa powder and almond milk thoroughly together (if you don't have a blender, this can be done by hand, but requires a little work with a whisk)

Fold in oats. Cover and place in the fridge over night

Sprinkle almonds and berries on the cake batter mousse before enjoying

Calories: 260

Fat: 9

Carbohydrates: 28

Protein: 25

Dessert recipe 3

Banana muffins

Bananas are a great source of energy, so this muffin can replace your breakfast, if you are into sugary injections in the morning.

Ingredients:

1 large ripe banana
¾ cup of egg whites
¾ cup whole wheat flour
½ cup plain Greek yogurt
1 tsp. baking soda
1 tsp. baking powder
½ tsp. cinnamon
Optional: walnuts, chocolate chips, etc.

Preheat the oven to 350. Add all ingredient to a food processor and blend until smooth.

Spray a muffin tin with non-stick spray.

Scoop about ⅓ cup of batter into each muffin tin.

Bake for 11-13 minutes or until a toothpick comes out clean.

Total Fat 4g

Saturated Fat 1g

Cholesterol less than 5mg

Sodium 180mg

Potassium 220mg

Carbohydrate 11g

Dietary Fiber 2g

Sugars 3g

Protein 8g

Dessert recipe 4

Cinnamon Raisin Balls

Raisin balls are hard to swallow if you don't know how to make them. This is the real deal.

Ingredients:
1 C almonds
1 C raisins
1 tsp. Cinnamon

Rinse the raisins and almonds with some water. Toss them in a food processor with the cinnamon. When sufficiently mixed, form into ball or bar shapes.

Calories: 220.3

Total Fat: 12.1 g

Cholesterol: 0.0 mg

Sodium: 3.6 mg

Total Carbs: 26.7 g

Dietary Fiber: 4.0 g

Protein: 5.9 g

Dessert recipe 5

Fruity Egg white Crepes

Colorful and super easy to make, you will love these festive version of crepes!

Ingredients:

Crepe
1 egg white (or egg substitute)
1 Tablespoon of milk
1 packet sweetener of your choice, or honey

Topping
1/2 cup frozen fruit
1 packet sweetener

Crepe
heat a small frying pan over med/high heat
mix egg white, sweetener, and milk very well
spray pan with butter spray (or anything else to grease it).
Pour egg mix into pan, allow to solidify somewhat then fold in half (like an omelet) and cook until slightly browned and not runny

Fruit topping
Mix fruit and sweetener. Zap in microwave for 1 minute to

make a sauce.

Calories: 66.9

Total Fat: 0.4 g

Cholesterol: 0.3 mg

Sodium: 9.7 mg

Total Carbs: 12.0 g

Dietary Fiber: 2.9 g

Protein: 4.2 g

Dessert recipe 6

Peanut butter whip with chocolate

Your kids will love this recipe! Chocolate and peanut butter make a great combination, especially when you need a protein boost.

Ingredients:

2 Fudgsicles
4 TB cool whip
2 TB Peanut Butter

Melt 2 Fudgsicle pops in the microwave. Add 2 TB of peanut butter and blend until smooth. Mix in 4 TB of cool whip. Blend until smooth. Put in freezer for 15 minutes.

Calories: 139.9

Total Fat: 9.4 g

Cholesterol: 0.0 mg

Sodium: 104.7 mg

Total Carbs: 12.6 g

Dietary Fiber: 2.9 g

Protein: 6.0 g

Dessert recipe 7

Silky Chocolate Mousse

Chocolate is often vilified as "fattening," but its ingredient, cocoa, is a highly nutritious, low calorie super food.

Ingredients:

175g Greek yogurt
10g heavy whipping cream
2g cocoa powder
1/2 ripe banana or sweetener of your choice
1tsp. vanilla extract
Pinch sea salt

Blend everything in a blender. For a less silky texture you can use a regular whisk. This recipe can be made in 2 minutes.

Calories 250

Protein 18g

Carbs 41g

Fat 5g

Dessert recipe 8

Sesame banana pancakes

When it comes to pancakes, there are few ingredients that cannot be used. This is a wonderful version with banana and sesame.

Ingredients:

For The Batter
1 peeled ripe banana
1/2 cup non-fat milk
2 tbsp. sugar
2 tbsp. whole wheat flour
2 tbsp. flour

Other ingredients:
1 tsp. oil for brushing
4 tsp. sesame seeds

To serve:
4 tsp. honey

For the batter

Slightly mash the banana and add milk and sugar to it. Blend in a mixer till smooth and fluffy. Transfer to a bowl and keep aside.

Add the wheat flour and flour to it and whisk well till smooth and lump-free. Keep aside.

Heat a non-stick pan. Brush it lightly with oil.

Pour 2 tablespoons of the batter and spread it to make a pancake. Sprinkle 1 teaspoon of sesame seeds on top and cook on both sides till done. Make 3 more pancakes with the remaining batter.

Serve hot with honey.

Carbohydrates: 23 mg

Cholesterol: 0 mg

Calories: 144

Fat: 4.2 mg

Fiber: 0.6 mg

Protein: 3.2 mg

Dessert recipe 9

Vanilla waffles

Your favorite classic waffle recipe with a tasteful vanilla twist. Crowd-pleasing and easy to make!

Ingredients:

For 4 waffles:
4 eggs
15 g coconut oil
25 g coconut flour
20 g arrowroot
1 teaspoon vanilla extract
1/2 teaspoon baking powder

Instructions:

Mix all the ingredients together and bake in a waffle iron.

Calories: 128

Protein: 7.1

Carbs: 5.3

Sugar: 0.5

Fat: 8.7

Fiber: 2.5

Dessert recipe 10

Lupin muffins

If this is your first time using lupin flour, you will be surprised the difference it makes! It is healthy and tastes great.

Ingredients:

For 4 muffins:
1 banana (100 g banana flesh)
1 egg
2 packs vanilla sugar (16 g) or you favorite sweetener
25 g coconut oil
45 g lupin flour
20 g arrow root
1 tsp. baking powder
30 g chocolate chips

Beat banana, egg and vanilla sugar in a blender. Melt coconut oil and add to mixture. Incorporate lupin flour, arrow root, and baking powder. Add chocolate chips by hand. Bake at 200 degrees Celsius until muffin tops look firm.

Calories: 200

Protein: 7.1

Carbs: 16.5

Sugar: 7.8

Fat: 11.6

Fiber: 5.4

Dessert recipe 11

Odd brownies

Sour and sweet brownies? Why not! This is a strange but delicious twist on your favorite brownies.

Ingredients:

1 (15 ounce) black beans
3 eggs
1/3 cup of melted butter, plus extra to grease baking pan
1/4 cup of cocoa powder
1 pinch of salt
2 teaspoons pure vanilla extract
1/2 cup cane sugar
1/2 cup semi-sweet chocolate chips
Optional: 1/3 cup of walnuts or other nuts of choice

Preheat oven to 350 degrees. Butter a baking pan. Combine the black beans, eggs, cocoa powder, salt, vanilla extract and sugar into a food process or blender. Gently stir in the chocolate chips (and nuts, if desired). Pour the mixture into the greased baking pan. Bake for 30 to 35 minutes at 350 degrees until the center is cooked. Let cool before cutting into squares.

Calories: 160

Total fat: 9g

Cholesterol: 50mg

Sodium: 35mg

Carbs: 17g

Fiber: 2g

Protein: 4g

Sugar: 12g

Dessert recipe 12

Raw chocolate pies

Dates and chocolate in a dessert can make wonders! This is a classic but delicious dessert!

Ingredients:

1 cup raw almonds
1 cup pitted dates
1/3 cup raw walnuts
1/3 cup cocoa or cacao powder
1/8 tsp. salt
1 tbsp. water
2 frozen over-ripe bananas blended with 2 tbsp. cacao or cocoa powder, 1/4 tsp. pure vanilla extract, and optional 2 tbsp. coconut butter or avocado.

Combine the nuts, dates, 1/3 cup cocoa, and salt in a high-quality food processor. Process until fine crumbles form. Add no more than 2 tbsp. water to achieve slightly-sticky dough, then process again until it sticks together in one big ball. If it's not yet sticky, simply process longer. Break off pieces with your hands and mold along the edges of mini muffin cups, pressing down in the middle to form a cup shape. Freeze at least 20 minutes or until ready to serve. Make the cream right before serving.

Calories: 84

Total fat: 5.5g

Sodium: 20mg

Carbs: 8.7g

Protein: 2.7g

Dessert recipe 13

Nut and fruit yogurt

This flavorful yogurt can substitute your breakfast as it is packed with health. Literally, it will keep you full until lunch!

Ingredients:

3 tbsp. chopped mixed nuts
1 tbsp. sunflower seed
1 tbsp. pumpkin seed
1 sliced banana
1-2 handfuls berries
200g vanilla yogurt

Mix the nuts, sunflower seeds and pumpkin seeds. Mix the sliced banana and berries. Layer up in a bowl with yoghurt and enjoy.

Calories: 69

Protein: 28g

Carbs: 53.g

Fat: 41g

Fiber: 6g

Sugar: 45g

Dessert recipe 14

Lemon cake

Summery lemon cake is a perfect birthday cake, if you ask me.

Ingredients:

225g unsalted butter, softened
225g brown sugar
4 eggs
Finely grated zest 1 lemon
225g self-rising flour
For the drizzle topping
Juice 1½ lemons
85g caster sugar

Heat oven to 180C. Beat together 225g softened unsalted butter and225g caster sugar until pale and creamy, and then add 4 eggs, one at a time, slowly mixing through. Sift in 225g flour, then add the finely grated zest of 1 lemon and mix until well combined. Line a loaf tin with greaseproof paper, then spoon in the mixture and level the top with a spoon.

Bake for 45-50 minutes until a thin skewer inserted into the center of the cake comes out clean. While the cake is cooling in its tin, mix together the juice of 1 1/2 lemons and 85g caster sugar to make the drizzle. Prick the warm cake all over with a skewer or fork, then pour over the drizzle – the juice will sink in and the sugar will form a lovely, crisp topping. Leave in the tin until completely cool, then remove and serve. Will keep in an airtight container for 3-4 days, or freeze for up to 1 month.

Calories: 399

Protein: 5g

Carbs: 50g

Fat: 21g

Fiber: 1g

Sugar: 33g

Salt: 0.3g

Dessert recipe 15

Decadent brownies

This could easily be your Valentine's cake substitute. These brownies are decadent and absolutely delicious!

Ingredients:

140g ground almonds
140g butter, softened
140g golden caster sugar
140g self-rising flour
2 eggs
1 tsp. vanilla extract
250g raspberries
2 tbsp. flaked almonds
Icing sugar, to serve

Heat oven to 180C and base-line and grease a deep 20cm loose-bottomed cake tin. Blitz the ground almonds, butter, sugar, flour, eggs and vanilla extract in a food processor until well combined.

Spread half the mix over the cake tin and smooth over the top. Scatter the raspberries over, then dollop the remaining cake mixture on top and roughly spread – you might find this easier to do with your fingers. Scatter with flaked almonds and bake for 50 minutes until golden.

Cool, remove from the tin and dust with icing sugar to serve.

Calories: 411

Protein: 8g

Carbs: 35g

Fat: 28g

Fiber: 3g

Sugar: 21g

Salt: 0.5g

CHAPTER 7: HIGH PROTEIN SHAKE RECIPES TO INCREASE MUSCLE GROWTH

1. Oat & Almond Shake

Preparing time: 5 minutes
Servings: 3

1. Ingredients:

220ml milk
1 tablespoon almonds (grinded) (15g)
1 tablespoon oats (15g)
1 teaspoon maple syrup (5g)
½ teaspoon vanilla extract (2-3g)
2 tablespoon Greek Yogurt (30g)
30g whey protein

2. Preparation:

All ingredients go in a blender and are blend until the consistence is smooth.

3. Nutritional facts (amount per 100ml/entire composition):

Contains calcium, iron;
Calories: 111   Total Fat: 3.2g
   Calories from Fat: 29   Saturated Fat: 0.7g

Cholesterol: 21mg
Sodium: 58mg

Potassium: 182mg

Total Carbohydrates: 9.3g
    Dietary Fiber: 0.8g
    Sugar: 5.1g
Protein: 11.1g
Calories: 333

    Calories from Fat: 86

Total Fat: 9.5g

Saturated Fat: 2.1g

Cholesterol: 64mg

Sodium: 175mg

Potassium: 547mg

Total Carbohydrates: 27.9g
    Dietary Fiber: 2.6g
    Sugar: 15.3g
Protein: 33.5g

2. Peppermint Oatmeal Shake

Preparing time: 5 minutes
Servings: 5

1. Ingredients:

70g oatmeal
30g bran flakes
300ml milk
50g quark
½ teaspoon peppermint extract (3g)
30g ice-cream (vanilla/chocolate)
50g whey protein (chocolate)

2. Preparation:

Mix all ingredients in a blender until the composition is smooth.

3. Nutritional facts (amount per 100ml/entire composition):

Contains Vitamin A, calcium, iron.

Calories: 180
    Calories from Fat: 51

Total Fat: 5.6g
    Saturated Fat: 2.9g

Cholesterol: 30mg
Sodium: 111mg

Potassium: 179mg

Total Carbohydrates: 20.7g
    Dietary Fiber: 2.5g
    Sugar: 6.2g
Protein: 12.6g
Calories: 900

Calories from Fat: 253

Total Fat: 28.1g

    Saturated Fat: 14.4g

Cholesterol: 151mg

Sodium: 555mg

Potassium: 869mg

Total Carbohydrates: 104g

    Dietary Fiber: 12.4g

    Sugar: 31.2g

Protein: 63.2g

3. Cinnamon Shake

Preparing time: 5 minutes
Servings: 3

1. Ingredients:

240ml milk
¼ tablespoon cinnamon (4g)
½ teaspoon vanilla extracts (3g)
2 tablespoon vanilla ice-cream (30g)
2 tablespoon oats (30g)
50g whey protein

2. Preparation:

Mix all ingredients in a blender until the composition is smooth.

3. Nutritional facts (amount per 100g/entire composition):

Contains Vitamin A, calcium, iron.

Calories: 131
    Calories from Fat: 30

Total Fat: 3.3g
    Saturated Fat: 1.8g

Cholesterol: 42mg
Sodium: 73mg

Potassium: 158mg

Total Carbohydrates: 10.3g
    Dietary Fiber: 1g
    Sugar: 4.8g
Protein: 15.3g
Calories: 342

    Calories from Fat: 89

Total Fat: 9.9g

Saturated Fat: 5.4g

Cholesterol: 127mg

Sodium: 219mg

Potassium: 474mg

Total Carbohydrates: 31g
    Dietary Fiber: 3.1g
    Sugar: 14.4g
Protein: 45.9g

4. Almonds Shake

Preparing time: 5 minutes
Servings: 5

1. Ingredients:

220ml almond milk
120g oatmeal
50g whey protein
80g raisins
20g almonds (grinded)
1 tablespoon peanut butter (15g)

2. Preparation:

Mix all ingredients in a blender until the composition is smooth.

3. Nutritional facts (amount per 100g/entire composition):

Contains : Vitamin C, iron, calcium.

Calories: 241
    Calories from Fat: 61

Total Fat: 6.7g
    Saturated Fat: 1.6g

Cholesterol: 24mg
Sodium: 57mg

Potassium: 339mg

Total Carbohydrates: 33.8g
    Dietary Fiber: 3.7g
    Sugar: 12.5g
Protein: 13.9g

Calories: 1207

    Calories from Fat: 304

Total Fat: 33.7g

Saturated Fat: 8g

Cholesterol: 122mg

Sodium: 283mg

Potassium: 1693mg

Total Carbohydrates: 169g
    Dietary Fiber: 18.5g
    Sugar: 62.3g
Protein: 69.4g

5. Banana & Almonds Shake

Preparing time: 5 minutes
Servings: 5

1. Ingredients:

2 bananas
230ml almond milk
20g almonds (grinded)
10g pistachios (grinded)
40g whey protein

2. Preparation:

Mix all ingredients in a blender until the composition is smooth.

3. Nutritional facts (amount per 100g/entire composition):

Contains Vitamin A, C, iron, calcium.

Calories: 241
    Calories from Fat: 61

Total Fat: 6.7g
    Saturated Fat: 1.6g

Cholesterol: 24mg
Sodium: 57mg

Potassium: 339mg

Total Carbohydrates: 33.8g
    Dietary Fiber: 3.7g
    Sugar: 12.5g
Protein: 13.9g
Calories: 1073

    Calories from Fat: 659

Total Fat: 73.2g

Saturated Fat: 52.1g

Cholesterol: 83mg

Sodium: 109mg

Potassium: 1934mg

Total Carbohydrates: 78.7g
   Dietary Fiber: 14.8g
   Sugar: 39.4g
Protein: 42.8g

6. Wild Berry Shake

Preparing time: 5 minutes
Servings: 7

1. Ingredients:

30g strawberries
30g blueberries
30g raspberries
30g currants
500ml milk
60g whey protein
1 teaspoon vanilla extract (5g)
1 teaspoon lemon extract (5g)

2. Preparation:

Mix all ingredients in a blender until the composition is smooth. You can also add some ice cubes to the mix.

3. Nutritional facts (amount per 100g/entire composition):

Contains Vitamin A, C, iron, calcium.

Calories: 78
    Calories from Fat: 19

Total Fat: 2.1g
    Saturated Fat: 1.2g

Cholesterol: 24mg
Sodium: 50mg

Potassium: 119mg

Total Carbohydrates: 6.7g
    Dietary Fiber: 0.7g
    Sugar: 4.7g
Protein: 8.7g
Calories: 549

Calories from Fat: 131

Total Fat: 14.6g

   Saturated Fat: 8.1g

Cholesterol: 167mg

Sodium: 351mg

Potassium: 832mg

Total Carbohydrates: 46.9g

   Dietary Fiber: 4.6g

   Sugar: 33g

Protein: 61g

7. Strawberry Shake

Preparing time: 5 minutes
Servings: 5

1. Ingredients:

30g strawberries
100g Greek Yogurt
200ml milk
40g whey protein
2 eggs
20g sweetener (honey/ brown sugar)
ice cubes
1 teaspoon vanilla extract (5g)

2. Preparation:

Mix all ingredients in a blender until the composition is smooth.

The Greek Yogurt can have different aromas like vanilla or strawberry, or just be plain yogurt. It works will all flavors.

3. Nutritional facts (amount per 100g/entire composition):

Contains Vitamin A, C, iron, calcium.

Calories: 96	Cholesterol: 87mg
Calories from Fat: 32	Sodium: 65mg
Total Fat: 3.5g	Potassium: 131mg
Saturated Fat: 1.6g	

Total Carbohydrates: 9.2g
　　Dietary Fiber: 2.5g
　　Sugar: 3.4g
Protein: 11.3g

Calories: 508

　　Calories from Fat: 157

Total Fat: 17.4g

　　Saturated Fat: 8g

Cholesterol: 433mg

Sodium: 326mg

Potassium: 656mg

Total Carbohydrates: 45.9g
　　Dietary Fiber: 12.4g
　　Sugar: 17.2g
Protein: 56.6g

8. Strawberry Vanilla Shake

Preparing time: 5 minutes
Servings: 7

1. Ingredients:

100g strawberries
1 banana
1 teaspoon vanilla extract (5g)
1 tablespoon strawberries extract (15g)
50g oats
200ml milk
5 eggs
Ice cubes

2. Preparation:

Mix all ingredients in a blender until the composition is smooth.

3. Nutritional facts (amount per 100g/entire composition):

Contains Vitamin A, C, iron, calcium.

Calories: 112
    Calories from Fat: 39

Total Fat: 4.3g
    Saturated Fat: 1.4g

Cholesterol: 119mg
Sodium: 59mg

Potassium: 170mg

Total Carbohydrates: 11.7g
    Dietary Fiber: 1.4g
    Sugar: 4.6g
Protein: 6.1g

Calories: 782

    Calories from Fat: 271

Total Fat: 30.1g

    Saturated Fat: 10.1g

Cholesterol: 835mg

Sodium: 421mg

Potassium: 1189mg

Total Carbohydrates: 82g
    Dietary Fiber: 10.1g
    Sugar: 32.5g

Protein: 43g

9. Strawberry & Nuts Shake

Preparing time: 5 minutes
Servings: 4

1. Ingredients:

50g strawberries
50g mix nuts (chopped)
200ml milk
100g Greek yogurt
2 tablespoon oats (30g)

2. Preparation:

Mix all ingredients in a blender until the composition is smooth.

3. Nutritional facts (amount per 100g/entire composition):

Contains Vitamin A, C, iron, calcium.

Calories: 140
    Calories from Fat: 81

Total Fat: 9g
    Saturated Fat: 1.4g

Cholesterol: 1mg
Sodium: 80mg

Potassium: 125mg

Total Carbohydrates: 9.2g
    Dietary Fiber: 1.4g
    Sugar: 4.3g
Protein: 6.9g
Calories: 417

    Calories from Fat: 324

Total Fat: 36g

    Saturated Fat: 5.4g

Cholesterol: 5mg

Sodium: 321mg

Potassium: 499mg

Total Carbohydrates: 36.9g
Dietary Fiber: 5.5g
Sugar: 17.1g
Protein: 27.6g

10. Raspberry Shake

Preparing time: 5 minutes
Servings: 4

1. Ingredients:

50g whey protein
100g raspberries
30g strawberries
50g sour cream
200ml milk
1 teaspoon lime extract (5g)

2. Preparation:

Mix all ingredients in a blender until the composition is smooth.

3. Nutritional facts (amount per 100g/entire composition):

Contains Vitamin A, C, B-12, iron, calcium.

Calories: 116
    Calories from Fat: 41

Total Fat: 4.6g
    Saturated Fat: 2.6g

Cholesterol: 36mg
Sodium: 54mg

Potassium: 168mg

Total Carbohydrates: 8.1g
    Dietary Fiber: 1.8g
    Sugar: 4.2g
Protein: 11.4g
Calories: 465

Calories from Fat: 166

Total Fat: 18.4g

Saturated Fat: 10.6g

Cholesterol: 143mg

Sodium: 214mg

Potassium: 670mg

Total Carbohydrates: 32.5g
Dietary Fiber: 7.1g
Sugar: 16.8g
Protein: 45.5g

11. Blueberry Shake

Preparing time: 5 minutes
Servings: 6

1. Ingredients:

250g blueberries
50g sour cream
80g oats
100ml coconut milk
160g pumpkin puree
Cinnamon, nutmeg for sprinkle on top

2. *Preparation:*

Mix all ingredients in a blender until the composition is smooth.

3. *Nutritional facts (amount per 100g/entire composition):*

Contains Vitamin A, C, iron, calcium.

Calories: 140
    Calories from Fat: 62

Total Fat: 6.9g
    Saturated Fat: 4.8g

Cholesterol: 4mg
Sodium: 9mg

Potassium: 192mg

Total Carbohydrates: 18.5g
    Dietary Fiber: 3.5g
    Sugar: 5.7g
Protein: 3g
Calories: 641

    Calories from Fat: 371

Total Fat: 41.2g

Saturated Fat: 29.1g

Cholesterol: 22mg

Sodium: 56mg

Potassium: 1150mg

Total Carbohydrates: 112g
Dietary Fiber: 21g
Sugar: 34.4g
Protein: 18.1g

12. Peanut Butter Shake

Preparing time: 5 minutes
Servings: 6

1. Ingredients:

300ml almond milk
50g peanut butter
50g mix nuts
6 egg whites
1 teaspoon butter extract (5g)

2. Preparation:

Mix all ingredients in a blender until the composition is smooth.

3. Nutritional facts (amount per 100g/entire composition):

Contains Vitamin C, iron, calcium.

Calories: 236
    Calories from Fat: 191

Total Fat: 21.3g
    Saturated Fat: 12.2g

Cholesterol: 0mg
Sodium: 109mg

Potassium: 241mg

Total Carbohydrates: 6.2g
    Dietary Fiber: 2g
    Sugar: 3.1g
Protein: 8.3g
Calories: 1415

Calories from Fat: 1148

Total Fat: 127.6g

Saturated Fat: 73.1g

Cholesterol: 0mg

Sodium: 656mg

Potassium: 1448mg

Total Carbohydrates: 37.2g
Dietary Fiber: 11.9g
Sugar: 18.5g
Protein: 50.2g

13. Peanut Butter & Banana Shake

Preparing time: 5 minutes
Servings: 7

1. Ingredients:

250ml almond milk
2 bananas
30g peanut butter
5 eggs
2 teaspoons honey (10g)
1 teaspoon vanilla extract (5g)

2. Preparation:

Mix all ingredients in a blender until the composition is smooth.

3. Nutritional facts (amount per 100g/entire composition):

Contains Vitamin A, C, iron, calcium.

Calories: 191
    Calories from Fat: 126

Total Fat: 14g
    Saturated Fat: 9.1g

Cholesterol: 117mg
Sodium: 70mg

Potassium: 288mg

Total Carbohydrates: 12.5g
    Dietary Fiber: 1.9g
    Sugar: 7.7g
Protein: 6.2g

Calories: 1339

    Calories from Fat: 884

Total Fat: 98.2g

Saturated Fat: 63.9g

Cholesterol: 818mg

Sodium: 487mg

Potassium: 2015mg

Total Carbohydrates: 87.6g

Dietary Fiber: 13.5g

Sugar: 53.9g

Protein: 43.6g

14. Peanut Butter & Chocolate Shake

Preparing time: 5 minutes
Servings: 3

1. *Ingredients:*

2 tablespoon cocoa powder (30g)
30g peanut butter
250ml almond milk
50g whey protein

2. *Preparation:*

Mix all ingredients in a blender until the composition is smooth.

3. *Nutritional facts (amount per 100g/entire composition):*

Contains Vitamin C, iron, calcium.

Calories: 326
    Calories from Fat: 240

Total Fat: 26.6g
    Saturated Fat: 19.7g

Cholesterol: 35mg
Sodium: 89mg

Potassium: 472mg

Total Carbohydrates: 10.6g
Dietary Fiber: 3.5g
Sugar: 4.3g
Protein: 17g
Calories: 977

    Calories from Fat: 719

Total Fat: 79.9g

    Saturated Fat: 59.1g

Cholesterol: 104mg

Sodium: 267mg

Potassium: 1415mg

Total Carbohydrates: 31.8g
Dietary Fiber: 10.6g
Sugar: 13g
Protein: 51g

15. Chocolate Shake

Preparing time: 5 minutes
Servings: 6

1. Ingredients:

3 tablespoon cocoa powder (45g)
250ml milk
120ml pumpkin puree
1 teaspoon vanilla extract (5g)
5 eggs

2. Preparation:

Mix all ingredients in a blender until the composition is smooth.

3. Nutritional facts (amount per 100g/entire composition):

Contains Vitamin A, C, iron, calcium

Calories: 89	Potassium: 185mg
Calories from Fat: 44	Total Carbohydrates: 5.6g
	Dietary Fiber: 1.4g
Total Fat: 4.9g	Sugar: 3g
Saturated Fat: 1.9g	Protein: 6.7g
	Calories: 534
Cholesterol: 140mg	Calories from Fat: 267
Sodium: 73mg	Total Fat: 29.6g

Saturated Fat: 11.4g

Cholesterol: 840mg

Sodium: 439mg

Potassium: 1112mg

Total Carbohydrates: 33.8g
Dietary Fiber: 8.4g
Sugar: 18.2g
Protein: 40.4g

16. Chocolate & Almond

Preparing time: 5 minutes
Servings: 5

1. Ingredients:

2 tablespoon chocolate pudding (30g)
50g almond (chopped)
300ml milk
40g whey protein
1 teaspoon amaretto syrup (5g)

2. Preparation:

Mix all ingredients in a blender until the composition is smooth.

3. Nutritional facts (amount per 100g/entire composition):

Contains Vitamin A, iron, calcium.

Calories: 131

Calories from Fat: 61

Total Fat: 6.8g

Saturated Fat: 1.4g

Cholesterol: 22mg

Sodium: 70mg

Potassium: 154mg

Total Carbohydrates: 9g
Dietary Fiber: 1.3g
Sugar: 3.5g

Protein: 9.9g
Calories: 656

Calories from Fat: 303

Total Fat: 33.7g

Saturated Fat: 6.9g

Cholesterol: 109mg

Sodium: 351mg

Potassium: 770mg

Total Carbohydrates: 45.2g
Dietary Fiber: 6.5g
Sugar: 17.2g
Protein: 49.3g

17. Caramel and Hazelnuts Shake

Preparing time: 5 minutes
Servings: 4

1. Ingredients:

50g hazelnuts (chopped)
1 teaspoon caramel syrup (5g)
1 teaspoon maple syrup (5g)
250ml almond milk
50g whey protein

2. Preparation:

Mix all ingredients in a blender until the composition is smooth.

3. Nutritional facts (amount per 100g/entire composition):

Contains Vitamin C, iron, calcium.

Calories: 307	Potassium: 326mg
Calories from Fat: 211	Total Carbohydrates: 15.5g
Total Fat: 23.4g	Dietary Fiber: 2.6g
Saturated Fat: 14.3g	Sugar: 11g
	Protein: 12.2g
Cholesterol: 26mg	Calories: 1228
Sodium: 37mg	Calories from Fat: 844

Total Fat: 93.8g

    Saturated Fat: 57.3g

Cholesterol: 104mg

Sodium: 148mg

Potassium: 1303mg

Total Carbohydrates: 61.8g
    Dietary Fiber: 10.4g
    Sugar: 44.1g
Protein: 49g

18. Plum Shake

Preparing time: 5 minutes
Servings: 8

1. Ingredients:

200g plum
50g raisin
200ml milk
4 eggs
100g quark
70g oats

2. Preparation:

Mix all ingredients in a blender until the composition is smooth.

3. Nutritional facts (amount per 100g/entire composition):

Contains Vitamin A, C, iron, calcium.

Calories: 122	Potassium: 149mg
Calories from Fat: 43	Total Carbohydrates: 14.7g
Total Fat: 4.7g	Dietary Fiber: 1.3g
Saturated Fat: 1.8g	Sugar: 7.2g
	Protein: 6.2g
Cholesterol: 87mg	Calories: 975
Sodium: 62mg	Calories from Fat: 340

Total Fat: 37.8g

    Saturated Fat: 14.3g

Cholesterol: 699mg

Sodium: 499mg

Potassium: 1190mg

Total Carbohydrates: 117g
    Dietary Fiber: 10.7g
    Sugar: 57.7g
Protein: 49.7g

19. Tropical Shake

Preparing time: 5 minutes
Servings: 5

1. Ingredients:

1 banana
150g pineapple
40g mango
200ml coconut milk
1 teaspoon honey (5g)
50g whey protein

2. Preparation:

Mix all ingredients in a blender until the composition is smooth.

3. Nutritional facts (amount per 100g/entire composition):

Contains Vitamin A, C, iron, calcium.

Calories: 178	Potassium: 294mg
Calories from Fat: 94	Total Carbohydrates: 15.3g
Total Fat: 10.4g	Dietary Fiber: 2.1g
Saturated Fat: 8.9g	Sugar: 9.9g
	Protein: 8.5g
Cholesterol: 21mg	Calories: 889
Sodium: 25mg	Calories from Fat: 468

Total Fat: 52g

    Saturated Fat: 44.6g

Cholesterol: 104mg

Sodium: 124mg

Potassium: 1468mg

Total Carbohydrates: 76.4g
    Dietary Fiber: 10.3g
    Sugar: 49.2g
Protein: 42.7g

20. Peach Shake

Preparing time: 5 minutes
Servings: 8

1. Ingredients:

6 peaches
300ml milk
140g mandarins
30g oats
4 eggs

2. Preparation:

Mix all ingredients in a blender until the composition is smooth.

3. Nutritional facts (amount per 100g/entire composition):

Contains Vitamin A, C, iron, calcium.

Calories: 70

Calories from Fat: 20

Total Fat: 2.3g

Saturated Fat: 0.3g

Cholesterol: 57mg

Sodium: 34mg

Potassium: 137mg

Total Carbohydrates: 9.5g
Dietary Fiber: 1g
Sugar: 7.2g

Protein: 3.5g
Calories: 839

Calories from Fat: 245

Total Fat: 27.3g

Saturated Fat: 9.7g

Cholesterol: 680mg

Sodium: 405mg

Potassium: 1639mg

Total Carbohydrates: 115g

Dietary Fiber: 12.4g

Sugar: 86.2g

Protein: 41.6g

21. Plum & Lemon Shake

Preparing time: 5 minutes
Servings: 6

1. Ingredients:

150g plums
2 lemons (juice)
2 teaspoons honey (10g)
200ml milk
Ice cubes
150g Greek Yogurt
4 eggs

2. Preparation:

Mix all ingredients in a blender until the composition is smooth.

3. Nutritional facts (amount per 100g/entire composition):

Contains Vitamin A, C, iron, calcium.

Calories: 74	Cholesterol: 85mg
Calories from Fat: 29	Sodium: 50mg
Total Fat: 3.2g	Potassium: 111mg
Saturated Fat: 1.3g	Total Carbohydrates: 6.4g
	Dietary Fiber: 0.6g

Sugar: 5.1g
Protein: 5.8g
Calories: 589

Calories from Fat: 228

Total Fat: 25.3g

Saturated Fat: 10.3g

Cholesterol: 679mg

Sodium: 397mg

Potassium: 890mg

Total Carbohydrates: 51.2g
Dietary Fiber: 4.6g
Sugar: 40.9g
Protein: 45.9g

22. Pineapple Shake

Preparing time: 5 minutes
Servings: 6

1. Ingredients:

300g pineapple
200ml almond milk
30g raspberries
30g oats
1 lime (juice)
40g whey protein

2. *Preparation:*

Mix all ingredients in a blender until the composition is smooth.

3. *Nutritional facts (amount per 100g/entire composition):*

Contains Vitamin A, C, iron, calcium.

Calories: 153	Potassium: 218mg
Calories from Fat: 80	Total Carbohydrates: 14.4g
Total Fat: 8.9g	Dietary Fiber: 2.6g
Saturated Fat: 7.4g	Sugar: 6.7g
	Protein: 6.6g
Cholesterol: 14mg	Calories: 920
Sodium: 18mg	Calories from Fat: 481

Total Fat: 53.4g

    Saturated Fat: 44.5g

Cholesterol: 83mg

Sodium: 109mg

Potassium: 1309mg

Total Carbohydrates: 86.3g
Dietary Fiber: 15.5g
Sugar: 40.3g
Protein: 39.6g

23. Orange Shake

Preparing time: 5 minutes
Servings: 8

1. Ingredients:

5 oranges
10 eggs
2 tablespoon honey

2. Preparation:

Mix all ingredients in a blender until the composition is smooth.

3. Nutritional facts (amount per 100g/entire composition):

Contains Vitamin A, C, iron, calcium.

Calories: 85

Calories from Fat: 29

Total Fat: 3.2g

Saturated Fat: 1g

Cholesterol: 117mg

Sodium: 44mg

Potassium: 163mg

Total Carbohydrates: 10.4g
Dietary Fiber: 1.6g
Sugar: 8.8g
Protein: 4.6g
Calories: 1189

Calories from Fat: 404

Total Fat: 44.8g

Saturated Fat: 13.8g

Cholesterol: 1637mg

Sodium: 618mg

Potassium: 2277mg

Total Carbohydrates: 146g
Dietary Fiber: 22.2g
Sugar: 123.9g
Protein: 64.1g

24. Pinna Colada Shake

Preparing time: 5 minutes
Servings: 8

1. Ingredients:

200g pineapple
200g coconut milk
50g oats
300ml milk
4 eggs

2. Preparation:

Mix all ingredients in a blender until the composition is smooth.

3. Nutritional facts (amount per 100g/entire composition):

Contains Vitamin A, C, iron, calcium.

Calories: 128

Calories from Fat: 75

Total Fat: 8.3g

Saturated Fat: 5.8g

Cholesterol: 76mg

Sodium: 48mg

Potassium: 149mg

Total Carbohydrates: 9.8g
Dietary Fiber: 1.1g
Sugar: 4.7g

Protein: 4.9g
Calories: 1155

Calories from Fat: 675

Total Fat: 75g

Saturated Fat: 52.1g

Cholesterol: 680mg

Sodium: 428mg

Potassium: 1339mg

Total Carbohydrates: 87.8g
Dietary Fiber: 12.2g
Sugar: 42.2g
Protein: 44.5g

25. Apple Shake

Preparing time: 5 minutes
Servings: 3

1. Ingredients:

350g apple
1 teaspoon cinnamon
200ml almond milk
2 teaspoon vanilla extract
40g whey protein

2. Preparation:

Mix all ingredients in a blender until the composition is smooth.

3. Nutritional facts (amount per 100g/entire composition):

Contains Vitamin C, iron, calcium.

Calories: 139	Potassium: 193mg
Calories from Fat: 77	Total Carbohydrates: 11.2g
Total Fat: 8.6g	Dietary Fiber: 2.3g
Saturated Fat: 7.4g	Sugar: 7.6g
	Protein: 5.7g
Cholesterol: 14mg	Calories: 833
Sodium: 18mg	Calories from Fat: 463

Total Fat: 51.4g

    Saturated Fat: 44.1g

Cholesterol: 83mg

Sodium: 106mg

Potassium: 1157mg

Total Carbohydrates: 67.3g
Dietary Fiber: 14.2g
Sugar: 45.5g
Protein: 34.3g

26. Egg Shake

Preparing time: 5 minutes
Servings: 8

1. Ingredients:

10 eggs
300ml milk
100g Greek Yogurt
2 tablespoon honey (30g)
50g oats

2. Preparation:

Mix all ingredients in a blender until the composition is smooth.

3. Nutritional facts (amount per 100g/entire composition):

Contains Vitamin A, iron, calcium.

Calories: 131	Potassium: 123mg
Calories from Fat: 55	Total Carbohydrates: 10.1g
Total Fat: 6.1g	Dietary Fiber: 0.6g
Saturated Fat: 2.2g	Sugar: 6.3g
	Protein: 9.1g
Cholesterol: 185mg	Calories: 1176
Sodium: 89mg	Calories from Fat: 498

Total Fat: 55.3g

    Saturated Fat: 19.5g

Cholesterol: 1667mg

Sodium: 799mg

Potassium: 1111mg

Total Carbohydrates: 91.1g
    Dietary Fiber: 5.1g
    Sugar: 56.3g
Protein: 82.2g

27. Pumpkin Shake

Preparing time: 5 minutes
Servings: 6

1. Ingredients:

300g pumpkin
300g raspberries
50g sour cream
200ml almond milk
40g whey protein

2. Preparation:

Mix all ingredients in a blender until the composition is smooth.

3. Nutritional facts (amount per 100g/entire composition):

Contains Vitamin A, C, iron, calcium.

Calories: 123

Calories from Fat: 72

Total Fat: 8g

Saturated Fat: 6.4g

Cholesterol: 13mg

Sodium: 18mg

Potassium: 238mg

Total Carbohydrates: 9.8g
Dietary Fiber: 4.1g
Sugar: 3.9g

Protein: 5.2g
Calories: 986

Calories from Fat: 576

Total Fat: 64g

Saturated Fat: 51.1g

Cholesterol: 105mg

Sodium: 146mg

Potassium: 1903mg

Total Carbohydrates: 78.2g
Dietary Fiber: 32.7g
Sugar: 31.2g
Protein: 41.7g

28. Beets Shake

Preparing time: 5 minutes
Servings: 6

1. Ingredients:

300g beets
50g parsley
80g blueberries
200ml milk
60g whey protein

2. Preparation:

Mix all ingredients in a blender until the composition is smooth.

3. Nutritional facts (amount per 100g/entire composition):

Contains Vitamin A, C, iron, calcium.

Calories: 89

Calories from Fat: 14

Total Fat: 1.5g

Saturated Fat: 0.7g

Cholesterol: 24mg

Sodium: 77mg

Potassium: 285mg

Total Carbohydrates: 10.3g

Dietary Fiber: 1.6g

Sugar: 7.2g

Protein: 9.5g

Calories: 531

Calories from Fat: 81

Total Fat: 9g

    Saturated Fat: 4.5g

Cholesterol: 142mg

Sodium: 464mg

Potassium: 1711mg

Total Carbohydrates: 61.9g
Dietary Fiber: 9.6g
Sugar: 43.3g
Protein: 56.8g

29. Coconut Shake

Preparing time: 5 minutes
Servings: 5

1. Ingredients:

100ml coconut milk
200ml milk
100g Greek Yogurt
50g whey protein
1 teaspoon coconut extract
30g coconut flakes

2. Preparation:

Mix all ingredients in a blender until the composition is smooth.

3. Nutritional facts (amount per 100g/entire composition):

Contains Vitamin A, C, iron, calcium.

Calories: 145

Calories from Fat: 78

Total Fat: 8.7g

Saturated Fat: 7.2g

Cholesterol: 25mg

Sodium: 48mg

Potassium: 184mg

Total Carbohydrates: 6.2g
Dietary Fiber: 1g
Sugar: 4.1g

Protein: 11.1g
Calories: 723

Calories from Fat: 391

Total Fat: 43.4g

    Saturated Fat: 35.9g

Cholesterol: 126mg

Sodium: 241mg

Potassium: 922mg

Total Carbohydrates: 30.8g
    Dietary Fiber: 4.9g
    Sugar: 20.6g
Protein: 55.8g

30. Mango Shake

Preparing time: 5 minutes
Servings: 8

1. Ingredients:

3 mango fruits
1 banana
50g strawberries
300ml milk
1 lime juice
6 eggs

2. Preparation:

Mix all ingredients in a blender until the composition is smooth.

3. Nutritional facts (amount per 100g/entire composition):

Contains Vitamin A, C, iron, calcium.

Calories: 87	Potassium: 155mg
Calories from Fat: 31	Total Carbohydrates: 10.3g
Total Fat: 3.4g	Dietary Fiber: 1g
Saturated Fat: 1.2g	Sugar: 7.8g
	Protein: 4.7g
Cholesterol: 101mg	Calories: 874
Sodium: 52mg	Calories from Fat: 306

Total Fat: 34g

    Saturated Fat: 12.3g

Cholesterol: 1007mg

Sodium: 524mg

Potassium: 1549mg

Total Carbohydrates: 103g
    Dietary Fiber: 9.7g
    Sugar: 78.5g
Protein: 46.7g

31. Watermelon Shake

Preparing time: 5 minutes
Servings: 6

1. Ingredients:

300g watermelon
200g cantaloupe
200ml water
1 teaspoon vanillas extract
50g sour cream
50g whey protein

2. Preparation:

Mix all ingredients in a blender until the composition is smooth.

3. Nutritional facts (amount per 100g/entire composition):

Contains Vitamin A, C, iron, calcium.

Calories: 59	Potassium: 154mg
Calories from Fat: 16	Total Carbohydrates: 5.9g
Total Fat: 1.8g	Dietary Fiber: 0g
	Sugar: 4.5g
Saturated Fat: 1g	Protein: 5.1g
Cholesterol: 16mg	Calories: 471
Sodium: 20mg	Calories from Fat: 128

Total Fat: 14.2g

    Saturated Fat: 8.3g

Cholesterol: 126mg

Sodium: 158mg

Potassium: 1230mg

Total Carbohydrates: 47.5g
    Dietary Fiber: 3g
    Sugar: 36.2g
Protein: 40.7g

32. Greek Yogurt Shake

Preparing time: 5 minutes
Servings: 6

1. Ingredients:

300g Greek Yogurt
100g coconut milk
2 tablespoon honey (30g)
40g raisin
200ml almond milk

2. Preparation:

Mix all ingredients in a blender until the composition is smooth.

3. Nutritional facts (amount per 100g/entire composition):

Contains Vitamin A, C, iron, calcium.

Calories: 167

Calories from Fat: 101

Total Fat: 11.2g

Saturated Fat: 9.8g

Cholesterol: 2mg

Sodium: 21mg

Potassium: 220mg

Total Carbohydrates: 13.6g

Dietary Fiber: 1.2g

Sugar: 11.5g

Protein: 5.5g

Calories: 1169

Calories from Fat: 706

Total Fat: 78.4g

    Saturated Fat: 68.5g

Cholesterol: 15mg

Sodium: 149mg

Potassium: 1541mg

Total Carbohydrates: 95.1g
    Dietary Fiber: 8.2g
    Sugar: 80.3g

Protein: 38.3g

33. Coffee & Banana Shake

Preparing time: 5 minutes
Servings: 6

1. Ingredients:

25g coffee (grinder)
2 bananas
150ml almond milk
20g peanut butter
100ml water
5 eggs

2. Preparation:

Mix all ingredients in a blender until the composition is smooth.

3. Nutritional facts (amount per 100g/entire composition):

Contains Vitamin A, C, iron, calcium.

Calories: 142

Calories from Fat: 89

Total Fat: 9.9g

Saturated Fat: 5.9g

Cholesterol: 117mg

Sodium: 61mg

Potassium: 240mg

Total Carbohydrates: 9.7g
Dietary Fiber: 1.5g
Sugar: 5.4g

Protein: 5.5g
Calories: 992

Calories from Fat: 621

Total Fat: 69g

    Saturated Fat: 41.4g

Cholesterol: 818mg

Sodium: 429mg

Potassium: 1683mg

Total Carbohydrates: 68g
    Dietary Fiber: 10.7g
    Sugar: 37.5g
Protein: 38.8g

34. Spinach Shake

Preparing time: 5 minutes
Servings: 7

1. Ingredients:

200g spinach
50g parsley
70g raspberries
200ml milk
100ml water
50g sour cream
50g whey protein

2. Preparation:

Mix all ingredients in a blender until the composition is smooth.

3. Nutritional facts (amount per 100g/entire composition):

Contains Vitamin A, C, iron, calcium.

Calories: 72	Sodium: 58mg
Calories from Fat: 25	Potassium: 282mg
Total Fat: 2.8g	Total Carbohydrates: 5.3g
Saturated Fat: 1.5g	Dietary Fiber: 1.5g
	Sugar: 2.2g
Cholesterol: 20mg	Protein: 7.4g
	Calories: 504

Calories from Fat: 174

Total Fat: 19.3g

    Saturated Fat: 10.8g

Cholesterol: 143mg

Sodium: 403mg

Potassium: 1973mg

Total Carbohydrates: 37g
    Dietary Fiber: 10.6g
    Sugar: 15.2g

Protein: 52.1g

35. Chia Shake

Preparing time: 5 minutes
Servings: 5

1. Ingredients:

100g chia seeds
200ml almond milk
50 sour cream
50g parsley
100ml water
40g whey protein

2. Preparation:

Mix all ingredients in a blender until the composition is smooth.

3. Nutritional facts (amount per 100g/entire composition):

Contains Vitamin A, C, iron, calcium.

Calories: 174

   Calories from Fat: 123

Total Fat: 13.7g

   Saturated Fat: 10g

Cholesterol: 20mg

Sodium: 30mg

Potassium: 260mg

Total Carbohydrates: 6.2g
   Dietary Fiber: 3.3g
   Sugar: 1.7g

Protein: 8.4g

Calories: 872

   Calories from Fat: 615

Total Fat: 68.3g

    Saturated Fat: 50.1g

Cholesterol: 99mg

Sodium: 152mg

Potassium: 1300mg

Total Carbohydrates: 31.2g
    Dietary Fiber: 16.5g
    Sugar: 8.5g
Protein: 42.1g

36. Papaya Shake

Preparing time: 5 minutes
Servings: 6

1. Ingredients:

3 papaya fruits
50g oats
300ml milk
1 teaspoon vanillas extract
50g whey protein

2. Preparation:

Mix all ingredients in a blender until the composition is smooth.

3. Nutritional facts (amount per 100g/entire composition):

Contains Vitamin A, C, iron, calcium.

Calories: 95

Calories from Fat: 14

Total Fat: 1.6g

Saturated Fat: 0.7g

Cholesterol: 16mg

Sodium: 34mg

Potassium: 81mg

Total Carbohydrates: 14.1g
Dietary Fiber: 1.4g
Sugar: 5.4g
Protein: 6.5g
Calories: 760

Calories from Fat: 113

Total Fat: 12.6g

    Saturated Fat: 5.9g

Cholesterol: 130mg

Sodium: 268mg

Potassium: 648mg

Total Carbohydrates: 113g
Dietary Fiber: 11.1g
Sugar: 43.5g
Protein: 52.4g

37. Vanilla & Avocado Shake

Preparing time: 5 minutes
Servings: 8

1. Ingredients:

3 avocados
20g vanilla sugar
150ml milk
200ml water
1 teaspoon vanilla extract
40g whey protein (vanilla)

2. Preparation:

Mix all ingredients in a blender until the composition is smooth.

3. Nutritional facts (amount per 100g/entire composition):

Contains Vitamin A, C, iron, calcium.

Calories: 155

Calories from Fat: 111

Total Fat: 12.3g

Saturated Fat: 2.8g

Cholesterol: 10mg

Sodium: 19mg

Potassium: 325mg

Total Carbohydrates: 8.5g
Dietary Fiber: 4g
Sugar: 3.2g

Protein: 4.5g

Calories: 1549

Calories from Fat: 1108

Total Fat: 123.1g

    Saturated Fat: 27.8g

Cholesterol: 96mg

Sodium: 187mg

Potassium: 3248mg

Total Carbohydrates: 84.8g
Dietary Fiber: 40.4g
Sugar: 31.7g
Protein: 45.1g

38. Cherry & Almonds Shake

Preparing time: 5 minutes
Servings: 8

1. Ingredients:

300g cherries
100g almond milk
6 eggs
30g almonds (chopped)
75g sour cream
200g milk
1 tablespoon vanillas extract

2. Preparation:

Mix all ingredients in a blender until the composition is smooth.

3. Nutritional facts (amount per 100g/entire composition):

Contains Vitamin A, C, iron, calcium.

Calories: 158

   Calories from Fat: 85

Total Fat: 9.5g

   Saturated Fat: 4.8g

Cholesterol: 115mg

Sodium: 64mg

Potassium: 155mg

Total Carbohydrates: 12.5g
Dietary Fiber: 0.9g
Sugar: 1.9g
Protein: 5.8g

Calories: 1424

    Calories from Fat: 766

Total Fat: 85.1g

    Saturated Fat: 42.8g

Cholesterol: 1031mg

Sodium: 574mg

Potassium: 1394mg

Total Carbohydrates: 113g
    Dietary Fiber: 7.8g
    Sugar: 17.4g
Protein: 51.9g

39. Carrot Shake

Preparing time: 5 minutes
Servings: 8

1. Ingredients:

300g carrots
200g strawberries
30g parsley
200ml milk
50g coconut milk
30g oats
5 eggs

2. Preparation:

Mix all ingredients in a blender until the composition is smooth.

3. Nutritional facts (amount per 100g/entire composition):

Contains Vitamin A, C, iron, calcium.

Calories: 84

Sodium: 64mg

Calories from Fat: 37

Potassium: 208mg

Total Fat: 4.1g

Total Carbohydrates: 8.2g

Saturated Fat: 2g

Dietary Fiber: 1.7g
Sugar: 3.8g

Cholesterol: 84mg

Protein: 4.4g
Calories: 844

Calories from Fat: 367

Total Fat: 40.8g

    Saturated Fat: 20.3g

Cholesterol: 835mg

Sodium: 640mg

Potassium: 2085mg

Total Carbohydrates: 81.7g
Dietary Fiber: 16.5g
Sugar: 37.8g
Protein: 44.2g

40. Grape Shake

Preparing time: 5 minutes
Servings: 8

1. Ingredients:

400g grapes
50g blueberries
200ml milk
100g Greek Yogurt
1 tablespoon vanilla extract
50g whey protein

2. Preparation:

Mix all ingredients in a blender until the composition is smooth.

3. Nutritional facts (amount per 100g/entire composition):

Contains Vitamin A, C, iron, calcium.

Calories: 88

Calories from Fat: 12

Total Fat: 1.4g

Saturated Fat: 0.8g

Cholesterol: 16mg

Sodium: 29mg

Potassium: 171mg

Total Carbohydrates: 12.2g
Dietary Fiber: 0.6g
Sugar: 10.8g
Protein: 6.9g
Calories: 706

Calories from Fat: 97

Total Fat: 10.8g

    Saturated Fat: 6g

Cholesterol: 126mg

Sodium: 229mg

Potassium: 1364mg

Total Carbohydrates: 97.6g
    Dietary Fiber: 4.8g
    Sugar: 86.4g
Protein: 55.4g

41. Cashew and Cacao Shake

Preparing time: 5 minutes
Servings: 4

1. Ingredients:

50g cashew (chopped)
2 tablespoon cacao powder (30g)
100ml almond milk
200ml water
50g whey protein (chocolate)

2. Preparation:

Mix all ingredients in a blender until the composition is smooth.

3. Nutritional facts (amount per 100g/entire composition):

Contains Vitamin C, iron, calcium.

Calories: 197	Potassium: 209mg
Calories from Fat: 127	Total Carbohydrates: 10.7g
Total Fat: 14.1g	Dietary Fiber: 3.2g
Saturated Fat: 7.8g	Sugar: 1.9g
	Protein: 12.9g
Cholesterol: 26mg	Calories: 789
Sodium: 30mg	Calories from Fat: 507

Total Fat: 56.3g

    Saturated Fat: 31.3g

Cholesterol: 104mg

Sodium: 119mg

Potassium: 834mg

Total Carbohydrates: 42.9g
Dietary Fiber: 12.7g
Sugar: 7.4g
Protein: 51.7g

42. Kale Shake

Preparing time: 5 minutes
Servings: 6

1. Ingredients:

300g kale
50g parsley
1 lime (juice)
20g ginger
300ml water
50ml milk
50g whey protein

2. Preparation:

Mix all ingredients in a blender until the composition is smooth.

3. Nutritional facts (amount per 100g/entire composition):

Contains Vitamin A, C, iron, calcium.

Calories: 59

Sodium: 36mg

Calories from Fat: 6

Potassium: 300mg

Total Fat: 0.7g

Total Carbohydrates: 8g

Saturated Fat: 0g

Dietary Fiber: 1.3g
Sugar: 0.8g

Cholesterol: 14mg

Protein: 6.3g
Calories: 475

Calories from Fat: 52

Total Fat: 5.8g

   Saturated Fat: 2.6g

Cholesterol: 108mg

Sodium: 288mg

Potassium: 2402mg

Total Carbohydrates: 64.2g
Dietary Fiber: 10.5g
Sugar: 6g
Protein: 50.1g

43. Lettuce Shake

Preparing time: 5 minutes
Servings: 8

1. Ingredients:

300g lettuce
50g spinach
30g parsley
100ml almond milk
30g oats
5 eggs
300ml milk

2. Preparation:

Mix all ingredients in a blender until the composition is smooth.

3. Nutritional facts (amount per 100g/entire composition):

Contains Vitamin A, C, iron, calcium.

Calories: 88

Calories from Fat: 50

Total Fat: 5.5g

Saturated Fat: 3.2g

Cholesterol: 84mg

Sodium: 54mg

Potassium: 172mg

Total Carbohydrates: 5.6g
Dietary Fiber: 0.9g
Sugar: 2.3g
Protein: 4.8g
Calories: 880

Calories from Fat: 498

Total Fat: 55.3g

Saturated Fat: 32.5g

Cholesterol: 844mg

Sodium: 544mg

Potassium: 1716mg

Total Carbohydrates: 55.6g
Dietary Fiber: 9.3g
Sugar: 22.8g
Protein: 47.8g

44. Kale & Ginger Shake

Preparing time: 5 minutes
Servings: 6

1. Ingredients:

200g kale
20g ginger
4 eggs
50g coconut milk
100g Greek yogurt
200g almond milk
1-2 tablespoon honey (15-30g)
20g chia seeds

2. Preparation:

Mix all ingredients in a blender until the composition is smooth.

3. Nutritional facts (amount per 100g/entire composition):

Contains Vitamin A, C, iron, calcium.

Calories: 146	Cholesterol: 82mg
Calories from Fat: 93	Sodium: 51mg
Total Fat: 10.3g	Potassium: 292mg
Saturated Fat: 7.6g	Total Carbohydrates: 9.2g
	Dietary Fiber: 1.6g

Sugar: 4g
Protein: 5.9g
Calories: 1165

Calories from Fat: 740

Total Fat: 82.2g

Saturated Fat: 60.4g

Cholesterol: 660mg

Sodium: 410mg

Potassium: 2338mg

Total Carbohydrates: 73.7g
Dietary Fiber: 13.1g
Sugar: 31.6g
Protein: 47g

45. Cucumber Shake

Preparing time: 5 minutes
Servings: 6

1. Ingredients:

300g cucumber
50g parsley
80g cottage cheese
1 teaspoon lime extract (5g)
300ml water
40g whey protein

2. Preparation:

Mix all ingredients in a blender until the composition is smooth.

3. Nutritional facts (amount per 100g/entire composition):

Contains Vitamin A, C, iron, calcium.

Calories: 39

Calories from Fat: 5

Total Fat: 0.6g

Saturated Fat: 0g

Cholesterol: 11mg

Sodium: 55mg

Potassium: 137mg

Total Carbohydrates: 3.6g
Dietary Fiber: 0.6g
Sugar: 1g
Protein: 5.4g
Calories: 310

Calories from Fat: 43

Total Fat: 4.8g

    Saturated Fat: 2.4g

Cholesterol: 90mg

Sodium: 441mg

Potassium: 1092mg

Total Carbohydrates: 28.8g
Dietary Fiber: 5g
Sugar: 8g
Protein: 43.5g

46. Matcha Shake

Preparing time: 5 minutes
Servings: 6

1. Ingredients:

20g matcha
1 lime (juice)
100g Greek yogurt
5 eggs
50g parsley
50ml coconut milk
200ml milk

2. Preparation:

Mix all ingredients in a blender until the composition is smooth.

3. Nutritional facts (amount per 100g/entire composition):

Contains Vitamin A, C, iron, calcium.

Calories: 94	Sodium: 68mg
Calories from Fat: 52	Potassium: 148mg
Total Fat: 5.8g	Total Carbohydrates: 4.6g
Saturated Fat: 3.1g	Dietary Fiber: 0.7g
	Sugar: 3g
Cholesterol: 120mg	Protein: 6.8g
	Calories: 661

Calories from Fat: 367

Total Fat: 40.8g

Saturated Fat: 21.7g

Cholesterol: 840mg

Sodium: 477mg

Potassium: 1033mg

Total Carbohydrates: 32.1g
Dietary Fiber: 4.7g
Sugar: 21.3g
Protein: 47.6g

47. Broccoli Shake

Preparing time: 5 minutes
Servings: 6

1. *Ingredients:*

200g broccoli
50g parsley
30g spinach
30g cottage cheese
300ml milk
100ml water
4 eggs

2. *Preparation:*

Mix all ingredients in a blender until the composition is smooth.

3. *Nutritional facts (amount per 100g/entire composition):*

Contains Vitamin A, C, iron, calcium.

Calories: 59	Sodium: 71mg
Calories from Fat: 25	Potassium: 169mg
Total Fat: 2.8g	Total Carbohydrates: 3.9g
Saturated Fat: 1.1g	Dietary Fiber: 0.8g
	Sugar: 2.1g
Cholesterol: 76mg	Protein: 4.9g
	Calories: 526

Calories from Fat: 230

Total Fat: 25.6g

   Saturated Fat: 9.7g

Cholesterol: 682mg

Sodium: 635mg

Potassium: 1521mg

Total Carbohydrates: 35.2g
Dietary Fiber: 7.5g
Sugar: 19.4g
Protein: 44.4g

48. Kale & Banana Shake

Preparing time: 5 minutes
Servings: 6

1. Ingredients:

150ml coconut milk
70g kale
30g spinach
1 banana
40g whey protein
200ml water
Sweetener per taste (honey/brown sugar)

2. Preparation:

Mix all ingredients in a blender until the composition is smooth.

3. Nutritional facts (amount per 100g/entire composition):

Contains Vitamin A, C, iron, calcium.

Calories: 109

Calories from Fat: 59

Total Fat: 6.5g

Saturated Fat: 5.6g

Cholesterol: 14mg

Sodium: 26mg

Potassium: 260mg

Total Carbohydrates: 8.1g
Dietary Fiber: 1.4g
Sugar: 3.5g
Protein: 6g
Calories: 651

Calories from Fat: 352

Total Fat: 39.2g

   Saturated Fat: 33.5g

Cholesterol: 83mg

Sodium: 155mg

Potassium: 1562mg

Total Carbohydrates: 48.5g
   Dietary Fiber: 8.1g
   Sugar: 20.8g
Protein: 36.3g

49. Mango & Peach Shake

Preparing time: 5 minutes
Servings: 8

1. Ingredients:

2 mango fruits
4-6 peaches
300ml milk
50g Greek yogurt
40g whey protein

2. Preparation:

Mix all ingredients in a blender until the composition is smooth.

3. Nutritional facts (amount per 100g/entire composition):

Contains Vitamin A, C, iron, calcium.

Calories: 64

Calories from Fat: 10

Total Fat: 1.1g

Saturated Fat: 0.6g

Cholesterol: 11mg

Sodium: 24mg

Potassium: 153mg

Total Carbohydrates: 9.3g
Dietary Fiber: 0.9g
Sugar: 8g
Protein: 4.8g
Calories: 640

Calories from Fat: 101

Total Fat: 11.2g

Saturated Fat: 5.9g

Cholesterol: 111mg

Sodium: 238mg

Potassium: 1531mg

Total Carbohydrates: 93.4g
Dietary Fiber: 9.5g
Sugar: 80g
Protein: 48.3g

50. Green Shake

Preparing time: 5 minutes
Servings: 6

1. Ingredients:

100g parsley
200g kale
100g raspberries
1 teaspoon lime extract (5g)
200ml water
30ml milk
60g whey protein

2. Preparation:

Mix all ingredients in a blender until the composition is smooth.

3. Nutritional facts (amount per 100g/entire composition):

Contains Vitamin A, C, iron, calcium.

Calories: 62

   Calories from Fat: 7

Total Fat: 0.8g

   Saturated Fat: 0g

Cholesterol: 18mg

Sodium: 39mg

Potassium: 292mg

Total Carbohydrates: 6.8g
   Dietary Fiber: 1.8g
   Sugar: 1.2g
Protein: 7.7g
Calories: 435

Calories from Fat: 51

Total Fat: 5.6g

   Saturated Fat: 2.3g

Cholesterol: 128mg

Sodium: 271mg

Potassium: 2046mg

Total Carbohydrates: 47.9g
   Dietary Fiber: 12.8g
   Sugar: 8.4g
Protein: 54g

51. Guava Shake

Preparing time: 5 minutes
Servings: 6

1. Ingredients:

2 guava fruits
6 eggs
200ml milk
20ml coconut milk
20ml almond milk
1 teaspoon vanillas extract (5g)
Sweetener per taste (honey/brown sugar)

2. Preparation:

Mix all ingredients in a blender until the composition is smooth.

3. Nutritional facts (amount per 100g/entire composition):

Contains Vitamin A, C, iron, calcium.

Calories: 101

  Calories from Fat: 54

Total Fat: 6g

  Saturated Fat: 2.8g

Cholesterol: 143mg

Sodium: 68mg

Potassium: 191mg

Total Carbohydrates: 5.8g
  Dietary Fiber: 1.5g
  Sugar: 4.2g
Protein: 6.5g
Calories: 709

Calories from Fat: 377

Total Fat: 41.9g

   Saturated Fat: 19.8g

Cholesterol: 999mg

Sodium: 477mg

Potassium: 1336mg

Total Carbohydrates: 40.7g
Dietary Fiber: 10.6g
Sugar: 29.3g
Protein: 45.5g

52. Mulberries Shake

Preparing time: 5 minutes
Servings: 6

1. *Ingredients:*

300g mulberries
200g spinach
50g cottage cheese
300g milk
3 eggs
30g oats

2. *Preparation:*

Mix all ingredients in a blender until the composition is smooth.

3. *Nutritional facts (amount per 100g/entire composition):*

Contains Vitamin A, C, iron, calcium.

Calories: 67

Calories from Fat: 22

Total Fat: 2.4g

Saturated Fat: 0.9g

Cholesterol: 52mg

Sodium: 72mg

Potassium: 220mg

Total Carbohydrates: 7.5g
Dietary Fiber: 1.2g
Sugar: 4g

Protein: 4.7g
Calories: 672

Calories from Fat: 217

Total Fat: 24.1g

Saturated Fat: 8.9g

Cholesterol: 520mg

Sodium: 719mg

Potassium: 2204mg

Total Carbohydrates: 74.6g
Dietary Fiber: 12.5g
Sugar: 40.1g
Protein: 47.3g

53. Grapefruits Shake

Preparing time: 5 minutes
Servings: 6

1. Ingredients:

2 grapefruits
200g Greek yogurt
200ml water
30g sweetener (honey/brown sugar)
50g whey protein

2. Preparation:

Mix all ingredients in a blender until the composition is smooth.

3. Nutritional facts (amount per 100g/entire composition):

Contains Vitamin A, C, iron, calcium.

Calories: 61	Potassium: 132mg
Calories from Fat: 9	Total Carbohydrates: 10g
Total Fat: 1g	Dietary Fiber: 2.9g
	Sugar: 3.9g
Saturated Fat: 0.7g	Protein: 8.2g
	Calories: 425
Cholesterol: 16mg	Calories from Fat: 65
Sodium: 23mg	Total Fat: 7.2g

Saturated Fat: 4.5g

Cholesterol: 114mg

Sodium: 160mg

Potassium: 923mg

Total Carbohydrates: 69.9g
Dietary Fiber: 20.5g
Sugar: 27.4g
Protein: 57.3g

54. Melon Shake

Preparing time: 5 minutes
Servings: 6

1. Ingredients:

300g melon
200g Greek Yogurt
100ml water
20g sweetener (honey/brown sugar)
50g whey protein

2. Preparation:

Mix all ingredients in a blender until the composition is smooth.

3. Nutritional facts (amount per 100g/entire composition):

Contains Vitamin A, C, iron, calcium.

Per 100g	Entire composition
Calories: 64	Potassium: 195mg
Calories from Fat: 10	Total Carbohydrates: 8.8g
Total Fat: 1.1g	Dietary Fiber: 2.1g
	Sugar: 4.7g
Saturated Fat: 0.7g	Protein: 8.3g
	Calories: 445
Cholesterol: 16mg	Calories from Fat: 68
Sodium: 29mg	Total Fat: 7.6g

Saturated Fat: 4.6g

Cholesterol: 114mg

Sodium: 205mg

Potassium: 1367mg

Total Carbohydrates: 62g
   Dietary Fiber: 14.5g
   Sugar: 33.1g
Protein: 58.2g

55. Pomegranate Shake

Preparing time: 5 minutes
Servings: 6

1. Ingredients:

4 pomegranates
60g whey powder
200ml milk
1 teaspoon vanilla extract
20g sour cream

2. Preparation:

Mix all ingredients in a blender until the composition is smooth.

3. Nutritional facts (amount per 100g/entire composition):

Contains Vitamin A, C, iron, calcium.

Calories: 88

Calories from Fat: 12

Total Fat: 1.3g

Saturated Fat: 0.8g

Cholesterol: 17mg

Sodium: 24mg

Potassium: 233mg

Total Carbohydrates: 13.6g

Dietary Fiber: 0g

Sugar: 10.6g

Protein: 6g

Calories: 790

Calories from Fat: 108

Total Fat: 12g

    Saturated Fat: 6.9g

Cholesterol: 151mg

Sodium: 215mg

Potassium: 2093mg

Total Carbohydrates: 123g
    Dietary Fiber: 4g
    Sugar: 95.7g
Protein: 54.2g

56. Kiwi Shake

Preparing time: 5 minutes
Servings: 6

1. Ingredients:

100g kiwis
8 eggs
200ml milk
20g sweetener (honey/brown sugar)
100g Greek yogurt

2. Preparation:

Mix all ingredients in a blender until the composition is smooth.

3. Nutritional facts (amount per 100g/entire composition):

Contains Vitamin A, C, iron, calcium.

Calories: 93	Potassium: 130mg
Calories from Fat: 47	Total Carbohydrates: 6.9g
	Dietary Fiber: 1.9g
Total Fat: 5.2g	Sugar: 3.1g
Saturated Fat: 1.9g	Protein: 7.8g
	Calories: 743
Cholesterol: 166mg	
	Calories from Fat: 376
Sodium: 78mg	
	Total Fat: 41.7g

Saturated Fat: 15g

Cholesterol: 1331mg

Sodium: 626mg

Potassium: 1043mg

Total Carbohydrates: 55g
    Dietary Fiber: 14.8g
    Sugar: 25g
Protein: 62.2g

57. Kiwi & Strawberry Shake

Preparing time: 5 minutes
Servings: 6

1. Ingredients:

200g kiwis
150g strawberries
50g Greek yogurt
200ml milk
60g whey powder

2. Preparation:

Mix all ingredients in a blender until the composition is smooth.

3. Nutritional facts (amount per 100g/entire composition):

Contains Vitamin A, C, iron, calcium.

Calories: 78

Calories from Fat: 13

Total Fat: 1.5g

Saturated Fat: 0.7g

Cholesterol: 21mg

Sodium: 33mg

Potassium: 197mg

Total Carbohydrates: 8.6g
Dietary Fiber: 1.3g
Sugar: 5.5g
Protein: 8.3g
Calories: 543

Calories from Fat: 93

Total Fat: 10.3g

Saturated Fat: 5.1g

Cholesterol: 144mg

Sodium: 228mg

Potassium: 1382mg

Total Carbohydrates: 60.1g
Dietary Fiber: 9g
Sugar: 38.4g
Protein: 57.9g

58. Cantaloupe Melon Shake

Preparing time: 5 minutes
Servings: 6

1. Ingredients:

1 cantaloupe melon (500g)
200g Greek yogurt
1 teaspoon vanilla extract (5g)
100ml milk
40g oats
6 eggs

2. Preparation:

Mix all ingredients in a blender until the composition is smooth.

3. Nutritional facts (amount per 100g/entire composition):

Contains Vitamin A, C, iron, calcium.

Calories: 111

Calories from Fat: 45

Total Fat: 5g

Saturated Fat: 1.8g

Cholesterol: 143mg

Sodium: 72mg

Potassium: 121mg

Total Carbohydrates: 7.2g
Dietary Fiber: 0.7g
Sugar: 3.2g

Protein: 9g
Calories: 775

Calories from Fat: 315

Total Fat: 35g

    Saturated Fat: 12.9g

Cholesterol: 1001mg

Sodium: 502mg

Potassium: 846mg

Total Carbohydrates: 50.7g
Dietary Fiber: 5g
Sugar: 22.6g
Protein: 62.9g

59. Passion Fruit Shake

Preparing time: 5 minutes
Servings: 4

1. Ingredients:

6 passion fruits (peal)
50g strawberries
200ml almond milk
50ml milk
1 teaspoon vanilla extract (5g)
60g whey protein

2. Preparation:

Mix all ingredients in a blender until the composition is smooth.

3. Nutritional facts (amount per 100g/entire composition):

Contains Vitamin A, C, iron, calcium.

Calories: 171	Potassium: 272mg
Calories from Fat: 97	Total Carbohydrates: 10.1g
Total Fat: 10.8g	Dietary Fiber: 3.3g
Saturated Fat: 9.1g	Sugar: 5.2g
	Protein: 10.4g
Cholesterol: 26mg	Calories: 857
Sodium: 39mg	Calories from Fat: 485

Total Fat: 53.9g

    Saturated Fat: 45.4g

Cholesterol: 129mg

Sodium: 193mg

Potassium: 1361mg

Total Carbohydrates: 50.5g
Dietary Fiber: 16.7g
Sugar: 26g
Protein: 51.9g

60. Currants Shake

Preparing time: 5 minutes
Servings: 6

1. Ingredients:

350g currant
200ml milk
1 teaspoon peanut butter (15g)
7 eggs
100g Greek Yogurt

2. Preparation:

Mix all ingredients in a blender until the composition is smooth.

3. Nutritional facts (amount per 100g/entire composition):

Contains Vitamin A, C, iron, calcium.

Calories: 85
Calories from Fat: 36
Total Fat: 4g
Saturated Fat: 1.4g
Cholesterol: 117mg
Sodium: 59mg

Potassium: 167mg
Total Carbohydrates: 6.6g
Dietary Fiber: 1.5g
Sugar: 4.2g
Protein: 6.2g
Calories: 846
Calories from Fat: 326
Total Fat: 40.2g

Saturated Fat: 14.2g

Cholesterol: 1168mg

Sodium: 589mg

Potassium: 1669mg

Total Carbohydrates: 65.9g
Dietary Fiber: 15.4g
Sugar: 42g
Protein: 61.7g

OTHER GREAT TITLES BY THIS AUTHOR

Advanced Mental Toughness Training for Bodybuilders

Using Visualization to Push Yourself to the Limit

By

Joseph Correa

Certified Sports Nutritionist

Becoming Mentally Tougher in Bodybuilding by Using Meditation

Reach Your Potential by Controlling Your Inner Thoughts

By

Joseph Correa

Certified Sports Nutritionist